the Baker's Tale

CATHERINE BROWN

the Baker's Tale

ANGELS' SHARE®

The Angels' Share is an imprint of
Neil Wilson Publishing Ltd
303a The Pentagon Centre
36 Washington Street
GLASGOW
G3 8AZ

Tel: 0141 221 1117
Fax: 0141 221 5363
E-mail: info@nwp.sol.co.uk
www.angelshare.co.uk
www.nwp.co.uk

Cover design and typesetting by Belstane

ISBN 1-903238-38-2
Printed in Finland by WS Bookwell Ltd

Foreword

THE Baker's Tale is not just a book – it can be looked upon as a 'complete guide to baking' covering all aspects from the type of flour to use when baking, easy to understand recipes, through to guaranteed results. Very innovative and creative, it covers classical bread through to bread with a modern twist.

I would recommend this book to anyone, from the inexperienced cook to the professional chef – 'a must have book', and I will certainly have a copy on my bookshelf!

Michel Roux

The Waterside Inn
Bray
Berkshire
August 2002

Contents

PART ONE

Baking a Better Loaf

Up a narrow staircase and through the swing doors there is a bar and comfy sofas covered with throws in lively colours. Beyond is the restaurant, uncluttered, white linen, soft grey décor. It's 1989 and there is a zing to this new eatery – The Triangle in Glasgow's Queen Street – which has been set up by a band of maverick chefs and ambitious entrepreneurs with ideas of changing things for the better. For a brief eighteen months it creates a buzz as the most talked about new restaurant. Yet my most lasting memories of it are to do with neither the modish décor, nor the innovative food, but a basket of bread rolls.

At the time, I was restaurant critic for the *Scottish Field*, so asking questions was part of the job. 'Who made the rolls?' I enquired.

'Our pastry chef, James Burgess.'

As I remember, he came out for a chat and the reason for the fabulous bread rolls soon became clear. He was not a pastry chef at all but a master baker. How had he ended up in a restaurant? Why was it such a rare treat to get some decent bread to accompany a restaurant meal? You can find the answer to the first question in *The Baker's Tale*. For the answer to the second, read on.

The best thing since sliced bread

It is 1946 and the nation's women have coped with everything from riveting battleships to tilling the fields. Now they are back in their kitchens, only to be caught up in the daily chore of scrimping and saving to the dictates of their ration books. For another eight years the gastronomic pickings are lean and it is 1954 before they are free of rationing. No other women in Europe have suffered such a lengthy period of thrift, in some ways a useful lesson about not wasting food. But their obsession to search for the cheaper option carries on long after the war is over. It has become their mantra. And in the decades that follow it will influence the way their food is produced,

made, packaged and sold, including their daily bread.

Since 1942 this has been based on a Ministry of Food ruling to millers and bakers, aimed at reducing wheat imports by making most use of the whole-wheat grain. The National Loaf was created for this purpose but it is not popular and by 1956 millers and bakers have returned to extracting all the endosperm and bran from the milling process to make a pure white flour loaf. In the interests of health, however, regulations are set up whereby minimum amounts of chalk (calcium), iron, vitamin B1 and nicotinic acid must be added to all flour with a high extraction rate. The all-white loaf is back on the bakers' shelves in its new form: sliced and wrapped. It makes such an impact that every good idea is subsequently known as 'the best thing since sliced bread'. What makes the bread the 'best thing', of course, is not its taste but its convenience and cheapness. Without washing machines, vacuum cleaners, spin dryers and electric mixers, these post-war women have their work cut out for them. They leap at anything that makes life easier and the sliced loaf is no exception.

Meanwhile, as the sliced loaf takes off, J Lyons sets up the first cornerhouse fast food outlets using a system of catering based on reheating frozen food in a microwave oven. The new oven has been discovered as a by-product of radar invention during the war. It has the perfect credentials for the fast food chain. It can reheat frozen food when required, saving on time and waste. Using mass-produced frozen produce there are high profit margins for the entrepreneur. Many copy Lyons, whose first Wimpy Bar (1954) is named after J Wellington Wimpy in the Popeye cartoon. In Omaha, Nebraska USA, an inventor, C A Swanson, patents the first frozen TV dinner which consists of roast turkey, dressing, giblet gravy, sweet potatoes and green peas. McDonald's hamburgers appear in 1955 and a year later the first Kentucky Fried Chicken (KFC).

Of price and speed (1960s)

A revolution in the food industry is underway, transforming the lives of the resourceful, scrimp-and-save, post-war women. By the end of the 1950s, more and more are able to afford labour-saving equipment. They are desperate to learn how to freeze food as they discover the convenience of refrigerators and deep-freezes (the first domestic microwaves are still a decade away). They are also discovering a new system of serve-yourself in the high street. The Co-op is the first to set up self-service stores. Soon there will be others. By 1962 there are 12,000 supermarkets. In 1964 Retail Price Maintenance collapses. Cut-price, special-offers, loss-leaders, pile-'em-high-and-sell-'em-cheap all join the retail jargon in a marketplace selling an increasing range of convenience foods at lower prices. Whether this can be described as the 'best thing since sliced bread' is a matter of opinion.

With growing affluence, another aid to women's liberation is the boom in eating out. Most opt for fast-cooked, convenient foods from take-aways and burger bars which are seen as a better bet – cheaper, of course, than unreliable hotels and restaurants charging what they regard as over-the-top prices. Raymond Postgate, who set up the *Good Food Guide* in the 1950s, confirms suspicions that most hotel and restaurant food is bad value for money. His guide criticises such dubious cooking habits as batch-cooking vegetables, hours before use; hot-plating, by which plates of food are kept in a hot plate sometimes for 20 minutes before they are served, the meat curling at the edges; cold joints, sliced thin, covered with hot gravy, and then served as roast meat. Pursuit of cooking the most food, in the shortest time for the least cost infiltrates every aspect of the food industry including the breadmakers.

Since the nutritious National Loaf has gone, there is a free-for-all in the baking industry. The British Baking Industries Research Association at Chorleywood in Hertfordshire is set up with a view to developing baking technology. This is funded, partly by the government, who are pressing research scientists to find ways of making British-grown wheat more acceptable for bread-making, thus saving on the cost of more expensive imported wheat. The other funding partners are the three giants in the baking and milling industry: Spillars, Rank Hovis McDougal and Associated British Foods.

For some time there have been voices arguing that sliced white is not, perhaps *'the best thing …'*. OK, the white flour is fortified with vitamins, but what's missing is the bran. These dissenters are distinguished medical and nutritional professionals who have become convinced, in their dealings with those in poor health, that missing out on bran is a bad idea. They believe bakery research should be encouraging bakers to make a more nutritious, better tasting loaf.

Chorleywood, however, is being driven by other factors more in keeping with the commercial mood of the times: speed and price. What they invent is unique. An entirely new method of making bread which becomes known as the Chorleywood Breadmaking Process (CBP). Its advantages include reducing the first 'bulk' fermentation period from many hours to a few minutes by using a fast dough mixer. It also uses much more yeast and bakes at a higher temperature than traditional breadmaking. Instead of taking 14 hours to make a loaf, it can be made in 90 minutes. It scores on time and produces a loaf that is good for sandwiches. But the new loaf does not have crisp crust, taste or texture. Like other foods produced in the interest of speed and cheapness, it has lost some of the quality and flavour in the process.

But as far as the innovative research scientists are concerned this is a small price to pay and they are delighted to have solved the technical problem of using British wheat. Many bakers are glad that they have access to some of the most modern bread technology in Europe. (The workers are pleased too that they can spend the night in their beds rather than in the bakery.) And, of course, women have the convenient, long-life bread they always wanted.

Like their attraction to mass-produced, cheap 'mousetrap' cheddar, British women also fall for mass-produced, cheap white bread with a long shelf life. This kind of bread (like the cheddar) is also welcomed by the newly powerful pile-'em-high-and-sell-'em-cheap super-markets. The plant baker's wrapped and sliced becomes the new National Loaf, finding its way into the supermarket trolleys of more than three-quarters of the British population. No other nation in Europe transfers its loyalties so wholeheartedly to industrialised bread.

The convenience revolution (1970s)

Since the early sixties, interest in food had been hotting-up but it reaches boiling point during the seventies. Soaring sales of cookery books, foodie TV programmes, endless restaurant guides, as well as gastronomic tours to all parts of the globe play an educational and motivational role. This coverage creates new needs, to which supermarkets and specialist shops respond with great speed. Combined with a government sympathetic to massive super-market development (unlike most other continental countries who restrict their expansion), it's a process that drives food production and multiple retailing forward more forcefully and more successfully than in any other European country. Other supporting factors include greater affluence and the rise of high-class restaurants and shops. While the Sunday supplements are making their mark, the expensive glossies too are gaining readers, constantly on the move up market as people make higher wages/salaries and work fewer hours, allowing them more time to experiment and enjoy themselves.

Post-war women who were once productive household labourers, toiling together as 'sisters', now have grown-up daughters who have become (along with men) consumers and public figures. This new, affluent generation of women with no reservations about price, are delighted to have speed and convenience in their cooking lives, until they begin to realise that there is a downside to their dream of a chore-free Utopia. Along with the discovery of sun-dried tomatoes and extra virgin olive oil, they learn the implications of the convenience revolution. Namely, that their daily food has been blasted by the scientific, agricultural, industrial and capitalist revolutions. Their gardens have been stripped, their kitchens sterilised. The market economy and the factory kitchen rules.

Some dissenters follow food writers and broadcasters who have a remit to report about behind the scenes in the food industry. They read about the poor value, in nutritional and environmental terms, of some of the food being produced. And what about their meat, fish, fruits and vegetables? It seems that the nature and source of the ingredients they buy is as important as seeking out the best flavoured olive oil.

Over-processed, over-priced convenience and ready-made food of poor nutritional value, some of them discover, may be damaging their family's health. And there are other questions about food safety. They join the movement, in revolt against everyone who tampers with food to the detriment of the finished product – including the national loaf. Newly suspicious consumers may still be in a minority, but in the decade which follows they are joined by others when their fears about food safety will be confirmed.

Hot and crusty(1980s)

A bread strike by plant bakery staff in 1978 causes a stir in the nation's bread habits. Queues form outside the remaining high street bakeries as customers regret that they have not been more loyal in the past. Bags of bread flour and yeast disappear from the supermarket shelves as fast as they can be replaced. Breadmaking at home is back in fashion. There is a growing movement that does not agree that sliced plant bread is 'the best thing ...'. Largely as a result of this upsurge of feeling, *The Sunday Times* launches its Campaign for Real Bread in 1980. As a result of media pressure, and consumer demand, there has already been a very effective Campaign for Real Ale alerting drinkers to the downside of industrial versus traditionally made beers.

During its year-long campaign, *The Sunday Times* publishes articles about bread, flour, yeast, millers and bakers. They also supply 5,000 high street bakers with a poster of British Breads to stick up in their shops. But possibly their most effective move is to alert consumers to such issues as the dubious tactic by supermarkets of using white bread as a 'loss leader' – selling it below its real price – while charging the full price for wholemeal. There is also, with the help of *The Sunday Times* readers, an investigation of the pseudo 'brown' loaf. This is not a loaf made brown exclusively with wholemeal flour but with a brown colouring added. This fact is not made clear on the label. Protests are made to the Minister of Agriculture, Peter Walker. Surely it is time the Government got the labelling laws sorted out to protect consumers from such deception?

Whether the *The Sunday Times* campaign has much effect on the mass of the population is doubtful, but they do claim credit for raising the consumption of wholemeal bread by 3% during their year-long campaign. This may also have been helped by The Vegetarian Society who have been running a Campaign for Wholemeal Bread since 1975. There is, certainly, no doubt that bread is a hot issue for many who care about the demise of good-tasting, slow-fermented, crusty bread. It has been a particular concern of one of the leading food writers of the post-war years who had already decided, in 1972, to investigate what was left of artisanal millers and their flours as well as traditional bakers and their breads. For the next five years she gathers everything she can find about flour and bread as it used to be.

Elizabeth David brought a breath of fresh air into the kitchens of post-war British women when she began writing about food in the 1950s. Her early books are about good, simple, peasant European food which she had discovered during her pre-war adventures in France, Italy and Greece. Though she was writing about foreign foods, she was also passing on a fundamental message about celebrating dishes that are appropriate to the country. Local rootedness in her native kitchen was her next concern. What about puddings, pies and potted meats? Exotic flavourings from a colourful colonial past? And what about bread?

When *English Bread and Yeast Cookery* is published in 1977, all journalists on national newspapers – along with a review copy of the book - get a Mrs David-baked, slow-fermented, crusty loaf made with stone-ground, unbleached flour. The real bread enthusiasts are ecstatic. Many new converts are enlisted. Meanwhile, sales of wrapped and sliced are falling – a matter of great concern to the industrial breadmakers. (By 1990 total bread consumption in the UK will fall to half the amount eaten in 1950, before the fast, industrial Chorleywood loaf was invented.) But for the moment the industrial bakers are considering the demand for a crusty loaf. They have an idea of solving their falling sales problem by finishing off their plant-made dough in retail outlets and in supermarkets. They set up 'live' bakeries which often use frozen plant dough with the added advantage, of course, during baking of sending 'heady aromas' of yeast baking around the stores. The 'hot bread' shop is born.

Hot and crusty it may be, but in her inimitable style Mrs David wonders if they will get away with 'charging extra for the pleasure of carrying it home unwrapped'. She goes on: 'For all that your bread shop may be decked out as a wholesome little old county bakery with smell to match, the dough has been made by methods very little different from the ones used in the great shining factory. And it is a fact of life that all bread, factory-made, homemade, good, indifferent and just plain awful, gives out a glorious smell when it's baking. To buy bread on its smell is asking for disillusion. How soon will the customers discover this? Will the make-believe bakers prosper? It will be interesting to watch the progress of the hot and crusty movement.'

A *divided market* (1990s)

The new 1990s consumers enjoy the convenience and freshness of hot and crusty bread. From 1995 to 2001, sales of in-store bread increases by 21%. But the big players, such as Allied Bakeries, Unilever and L'Art du Pain, are not content with their progress. Sales of bread generally are still dropping. Sales of the plant loaf continue to decline and they decide to push ahead with a new development of their successful 'hot and crusty' breads. They invest heavily in a new concept which takes baking the daily loaf into every convenience store and corner shop. This high-tech bakery system is known as 'bake-off' and brings baking into the fast food fold with products taking 12–20 minutes to produce. The products arrive in the store frozen and require no baking expertise to produce. Retail staff put them in a small oven and press a few buttons on a computer panel. The industrial baker provides a wide range of ready-to-bake morning rolls and breads and encourages retailers to exploit impulse buying by baking frequently throughout the day. That 'heady aroma' of wafting baking does the trick again. Growth is 25% per year and profit margins typically around 40%, though it is possible to make 53% with some speciality items. Pseudo 'hot and crusty' may be finding a ready market, but another type of bread has been rising in different ovens.

Working with an Italian master baker, recruited from Italy, Peggy Daggenbaum, an American mother of four with an MBA from the London School of

Economics, set up her first bakery in London in the mid eighties. She had lived for several years in Italy and had become interested in their rustic, every-day breads.

High street bakers in Italy have survived the onslaught of industrial baking by providing a more interesting loaf. Many are regional breads, previously unknown nationally. Italian bakers in the large cities have redesigned their shops with counters and display areas to accommodate a wide range of regional breads using unbleached flours and traditional baking methods. They are doing a roaring trade.

Moving to London to work, Daggenbaum immediately sees the gap in the UK market, and being first and foremost a businesswoman, decides to set up a bakery making Italian regional breads. Once the bakery, La Fornaia, is up and running she sets off with a selection of her breads to hawk around. She turns up at Marks and Spencer with a basket of interesting looking breads. As an afterthought she has put in an ugly looking loaf which originally came from around Lake Como. It is pale and floury and looks a bit like a squashed arm. Italians call it *ciabatta* (slipper) bread. Much to her surprise the M&S buyer takes a fancy to it. What it lacks in looks it makes up for in taste: a crisp crust, chewy texture, beautiful holes and satisfying flavour.

From obscurity, ciabatta becomes the cult bread of the 90s. Asked what she thought had contributed to its success, Daggenbaum explains: 'It's very tactile – you really want to feel this bread. Can you imagine anyone wanting to tear apart a standard British loaf?'

Unlike most other breads, *ciabatta* is made with a very wet dough and is not moulded but allowed to form its own shape on the baking tray. 'You brew it up,' she says, 'leave it alone for a few hours, shove it in the oven, and away you go. What it needs to taste good is excellent ingredients, a long fermentation time for the dough to mature and develop its flavour – and experience. And you won't get that from additives and dough improvers and the physical bashing given to modern bread.'

Ciabatta caught the mood of the times. Notable British bakeries who were already making real bread, like Andrew Whitely's Village Bakery at Melmerby in Cumberland, took up the opportunity and expanded as the world and its supermarkets beat a path to their door. Handmade breads, however, were still not so welcome in hotels and restaurants where the age-old system of hotel bread buying – a week's supply from the cash and carry at the lowest knockdown price – continued.

Pioneers who saw bread as an important menu item in its own right were few and far between. Caterers, generally, were reluctant to let people fill up on bread in case it inhibited their consumption of other more lucrative items later on in the meal. Finding an exception to the rule was rare. Which is where I came in at the beginning. Thankful to find Jimmy Burgess baking a better loaf.

The Baker's Tale

The start of a dream...

I suppose the start of my dream was when I left Dunblane Secondary school and started work as an apprentice baker to James Harper, Main Street, Callander, Perthshire. I left school on the Friday and started in the bakers on the Monday. It was 1951 and I was 14 years old.

How did I make up my mind to become a baker? Well, circumstances really. My mother and father had taken a job, together, in private service. It was the first time they had taken this kind of work together in the same house and it was a disaster from the start. One thing led to another and they got the sack. So both of them were on the move and the children, my brother, sister and myself went to live with my Gran in Dunblane.

Every morning, Gran took me to Brown's the bakers in the High Street. I was fascinated. Watching the bakers chaff (shape up) the scones and transfer them to the hotplate, I used to stand for a good 20 minutes each morning, sometimes talking to the bakers. So I guess this was what made up my mind.

James Harper was a first class baker and I learned a lot from him. I was more or less a dogsbody and for the first six months all I did was scrape pans and wash utensils. But I worked hard and listened. An old baker, Davie Ireland, took me under his wing and showed me how to work the hotplate (pancakes, scones, crumpets and potato scones). The wages, to start with, were 12 shillings (70p) a week.

During the time I was with Mr Harper, I was given my first lesson in life – to do what I was told. I was asked to take the macaroons out of the oven and I forgot. However, the bakery was a very happy place and I was sorry to leave when my dad moved again to Gartocharn between Balloch and Drymen.

I discovered there was a bakers, McGowan's, in Drymen, four miles away. So away I went and arrived at the shop, asking to speak to the boss. I gave him my reference from Mr Harper and asked for a job.

'OK,' he says, 'I'll start you at 15 shillings a week – 8am to 4.30pm. Saturdays 8–12pm.'

So here we go again, I thought.

Working here changed my life in many ways although I wasn't to know that at the time. This is where I first learned about fermentation and '14-hour' doughs. These were the doughs that were made up the day before and given a long fermentation to improve the flavour and texture. Also I learned how to make brown breads, puff pastry, pies, bridies, small cakes, sultana, cherry, and Dundee cakes as well as Abernethy, parkin and rice biscuits.

Though my mother and father moved on again, I stayed in Drymen, going into lodgings with Mrs Barrie. Her husband was a butcher and they really looked after me.

The baker enrolled me for a four-year course of Bakery Classes at the Royal Technical College in George Square (now the University of Strathclyde). First I had to pass an entrance exam in Bakery, Maths, Science and English. I really threw all my energies into the night classes (Mondays, Tuesdays and Wednesdays from 3pm to 8.30pm) though, of course, it meant I wasn't getting much sleep. But it paid off and I was passing my exams easily. The college was teaching me the theory of fermentation and other baking procedures as well as giving me the opportunity to perfect my practical skills making confectionery, gateaux and wedding cake decoration which I didn't get from Mr McGowan.

From baker to army caterer...

I was in my third year (with only 1 year to go) when I received a letter from the War Office telling me that I had to report to Aldershot for National Service. So this was the start of a new era.

For the first six weeks I didn't know what had hit me. One thing for sure, I did not like my thinking being done for me. However, this phase soon passed and things began to look up when I was posted to Blandford in Dorset to do my 'trade training'. This was where they taught you 'to cook'. Or so they thought.

Then I was moved to Glencourse Barracks in Edinburgh and this was better. I got on very well and every week I went home on a weekend pass. But all good things come to an end. One day we received word from the War Office that we were being posted to Korea! I believe I was the last British cook to go to Korea.

This was the beginning of another chapter in my life. They say things are 'tough on the road'. I was about to find out, though the boat trip via the Cape of Good Hope to Hong Kong was wonderful.

When we landed in Korea we were on long marches, sometimes three weeks away from base camp. War is never pretty. I lost my best pal. We were out in the 'field' and I bent down to ties my laces and next thing he was hit by a bullet and lying dead at my feet.

Gibraltar was our next posting and it was here that I began to have trouble with the authorities over the catering standards. The Army Catering Manual was the law. But what a load of 'guff'. No wonder folk 'went missing' from meals. Because I had experience as a craft baker, I was put in charge of the pastry. But making army pastry was like living with The Flintstones (they hadn't a clue).

However, I got to work and began to produce pastries that melted in your mouth, using different methods with the same ingredients. Soon, it came to the notice of the Colonel that attendance at meals in the main kitchen was increasing while elsewhere it was dropping.

But unknown to me, an investigation was being undertaken. They had caught me making milk puddings with six pints of milk instead of the two pints of milk and four pints of water which was the recipe in the army-catering manual. I was put on a charge: disrespect for the Army Catering Manual, and using army rations not laid down for the job. I was right in it, up to my neck. I told the Colonel what I thought of his Catering Manual and we agreed to differ. Just as long as I agreed to become the cook in the Officer's Mess.

1950s…back to a changed bakery world…

Soon the time came to return to 'civvy street' – a more mature and wiser person. I got a job with Hastie's of Cambuslang. It was a big bakery with several shops and vans and ran a system of deep freezing the produce. This was not really what I was looking for and after a year I was on the move again to a small home bakery in Jordanhill.

By this time I'd bought a motorbike so could stay at home in Kilmacolm with my parents and travel each day to work. I wanted to finish my baking training but what a shock I got. All the courses I'd been on had been discontinued. It was nearly four years since I'd left to do National Service.

Eventually I got back into another bakery course but had to start again at the beginning. It was a hard slog, but I was determined and single-minded. I'd managed to get a job in Lyons Bakery in Craigton Road where I met my wife, Margaret. I wanted to get my training finished so we could get married and asked the management if I could go 2 days a week full-time instead of 2 nights. Their reply was: 'no way'. So I handed in my notice.

A few days later the management asked to see me and apparently they had been making enquiries at the college and had decided to let me off for the two days. It was a great help and I obtained great results in all my classes.

But by this time it was the mid-1960s and the trade was going through a period of transition. It was becoming automated and I was never much use at the mechanical side of things. I tried a job in Bristol with a large cake making company but was not a happy chappy. So it was back to square one. Little did I know it but this part of my career, which I'd just, finally, got my qualifications for – as a craft baker, was coming to an end.

The bakery jobs I was getting were very poorly paid and I was becoming disillusioned with the trade. After all the struggle of qualifying to a very high standard, I was finding that bosses were not interested in my awards: only my labour at a cheap price. The last job I had before I quit was at Crawford's in Auchenshuggle, up by Celtic Football Club.

They made super bakery goods but the wages were the worst I ever had (on day shift £12.50 a week). After about a year, I took time off to go and see Margaret after she'd given birth to our eldest daughter, Caroline, and my wages for the week were cut to £9.50. It was the last straw and I quit baking in 1969 to go into selling insurance. I thought the bakery industry was bad, but insurance was three times worse. The hours were long. The pressure to sell insurance was intolerable. In the end I collapsed with a nervous breakdown. It was the end of insurance for me. I had worked in it for 11 years.

1980, what to do next?

When I was getting better I thought about trying to go to university, but in the end got a job as pastry chef in the old Albany Hotel in Bothwell Street. It proved to be a killer of a job, but I stuck it for four and half years, then packed it in and was unemployed for about a year. Nobody wanted to know me. In this trade sometimes it's not what you know but who you know.

Despite this, I decided to get some further catering qualifications and went to Glasgow College of Food Technology and then Ayr College to do an advanced City and Guilds 760/2 course. It was a pretty tough course, but I managed it. This was the beginning of the second part of my baking career.

I'd met David Cowan, he'd been a chef at the Albany, and he phoned me up to ask if I'd like to work as a pastry chef at a new restaurant, The Triangle, in Queen Street. It was 1989. At last I was beginning to see some light at the end of the tunnel.

Pioneering fresh restaurant-baked bread…

It was here that I was given scope to try out new ideas and made fresh bread every day for the restaurant. I had suggested to David that I could make bread when he was discussing the job with me. I never realised at the time what it would lead to, but things were good for me at The Triangle. It was a very happy place, and I was very happy.

We made rolls every day with different toppings. I made garlic bread in a baton shape. For desserts we made filled brioche, chocolate tarts, brandy snap baskets, crème brulée, ducat cakes, which were small yeast cakes cut into rounds brushed with butter, crisped on top and served with sauce

anglaise. Petit fours were truffles, decorated mints and I made my own chocolates. As a result we won a *Taste of Scotland* award and people were beginning to hear about us.

One Devonshire Gardens had just opened and Beverly Payne, the general manager, brought the owner, Ken McCulloch, as well as *The Herald* Food Critic, Raymond Gardner (Trencherman) to The Triangle a few times for dinner.

Unknown to me, Beverly and Ken were looking for new ideas. They were interested in improving the pastry department at One Devonshire. As it turned out, The Triangle was only a staging post for me since the owner got into financial difficulties. After about a year, the restaurant was closed and we were all out of a job. David Cowan moved to One Devonshire. After doing so well at The Triangle I was sitting at home wondering, what next? Then I got a phone call from David. Would I come for an interview with Beverly Payne?

Shortbread and tablet for the guests…

It took three minutes to agree the rise in wages and five to have a chinwag about the job. Then she asked me: 'Can you make shortbread? Can you make the bread for the restaurant?' No problems, I said. But you'll have to get me the right equipment.

Well, this was attended to, and away we went. Little did I imagine what adventures lay ahead. It was the beginning of the longest relationship I'd ever had with an employer.

All this started in April 1991. I got on well with Beverly. If you worked hard, she stood by you. And throughout the years this proved to be the case. Mr McCulloch wanted awards, so we were all kept on our toes. He was a difficult man to please. Staff turnover was high, and what was needed was a leader in the kitchen. The hunt went on for an executive chef who would lead the team in the right direction.

He arrived in October 1995. The minute I shook hands with Andrew Fairlie I knew that he was something special.

And everything I thought at that time proved to be true. He turned One Devonshire upside down till he brought it up to Michelin star standard. Of course, he didn't do it on his own; a very good team of chefs backed him up. And I am glad to say that I was one of them. It was a tremendous achievement.

When Andrew came and things got busier, the job of pastry chef was too much for me on my own – sometimes I was working 14-hour days – so a French pastry chef was employed to do the desserts. Then I was able to concentrate on the breads and rolls for breakfast as well as the cakes, scones and shortbreads for afternoon teas.

By this time I'd perfected my shortbread recipe. The original idea (using a proportion of cornflour instead of all flour, and icing sugar instead of caster, to make a more 'melting' shortbread) came from Mrs McLeod, an old lady I knew in Govan. She gave me the ingredients and I worked out the rest for myself. I gave her my recipe for Sultana Cake in exchange.

The tablet I was making was good, but I raise my hat to Gregor Mathieson's mum's tablet. He was General Manager at One Devonshire at the time and his mum had won a Women's Rural Institute world championship tablet award with her recipe. Again, she just gave me the ingredients and I worked out the rest for myself. When Andrew Fairlie came he wanted tablet and shortbread after lunch, petit fours after dinner.

Visitors began asking about the tablet and shortbread – Delia Smith, among other celebrities. They were like a plague of locusts. I could not keep them supplied. If you can imagine: 480 pieces of shortbread and 270 pieces of tablet a week. Billy Connolly was a special shortbread fan and I used to make up a few boxes for him to take away whenever he visited.

In addition to the bread and rolls, I added muffins, scones, doughnuts, soda bread and banana bread to the breakfast baskets. Andrew was under pressure to get his breakfast standards raised. He tried to lay out cheeses, cold meats etc. but it did not work.

I suggested we introduce muffins. Not the big ugly ones you see in American coffee bars, but tasty little apple, poppy seed, vanilla and sultana muffins. They went very well. So I introduced fresh scones and Devon splits, soda bread, fruit and banana bread each morning. I used to put a selection in each basket. It went a treat since Americans just love the sweet things for breakfast.

For afternoon teas, we had just been doing shortbread and scones but Andrew asked me if we could raise the standards here too. So we started giving four different types of sandwiches and freshly made scones with a pot of jam and cream, cream sponge, sultana cake or other cut cake, meringues, chocolate éclairs, strawberry tarts, Belgium biscuits and gingerbread. Afternoon teas went from 2 a month to 30 or so a week. If it was extra busy I could do up to 40 a day.

Another interest that I had been developing over the years was decorative sugar work. It's a specialist craft and I was delighted when ODG gave me an all expenses paid trip to work with Colin Martin, an expert in decorative sugar stretching and blowing, in the Lake District.

When I came back from this we were beginning to get into top gear. Awards were coming thick and fast and we were getting noticed. Then we hit the jackpot in October 1996 when we got a Michelin star. For the next four years things went very well under the guidance of Andrew Fairlie. A lot was achieved and the reputation of One Devonshire was at its peak. However in 2000, a year before I was due to retire, Mr McCulloch dropped the bombshell that he'd sold One Devonshire to Residence International, a company with no previous hotel experience. So big trouble ahead.

Three months before I retired, Andrew told me that he was moving on too. But, like the gentleman he is, said that he would see me retire first. They – including Residence International – gave me a great send off. A weekend trip to Paris, a portrait of One Devonshire, £200 in vouchers, a retiral lunch for my wife and I, and a bouquet of flowers for my wife, champagne and a car to take us home. Shortly after this, Andrew left. Now he runs his own restaurant within Gleneagles Hotel. Good luck and God bless him.

Postscript

There is no easy answer to success. Hard work and dedication you most certainly need to have. Also, I've never been afraid to ask advice. No one knows it all, but everyone is born with some sort of talent. The challenge is to discover what it is and then use it in the best way possible.

I think it's also important to pass on skills to the next generation. I have always been very keen to help young people in the industry who wanted to learn. I think this is why I'm still enjoying this kind of work.

No matter how experienced you are, you're always learning. I am still full of enthusiasm. I realise how lucky I have been to work with so many talented people in such a prestigious establishment as ODG. And in return for my hard work I've worked with and met many people who have paid me wonderful compliments. What more can a person want.

To all the following my sincere thanks

Andrew Fairlie, Stephen McLauchlan, J Hardie, Scott McCrae, Matthew Oats, C Williams, Tom Kuckove, J Watts (Michelin Star Winners). Also other pastry chefs I have worked with: Pierre Treaubalt, John Brett, James Hardy, Petra Brandholst, Colin Garvie, Barry Moran. Also thanks to Norman Robertson, Head Lecturer of Catering at Ayr College and especially his wife Sheena, who gave me my recipe for One Devonshire bread.

Ingredients

FLOUR

Flour is the ground meal of any edible grain. It may be made from a single grain or a mixture of different grains. It may also be ground in differing degrees of fineness/roughness and may be made from the wholegrain or just from the white starchy part of the grain. Usually the outer bran layer (husk) and endosperm (germ) are removed to make a finer flour, preferred for more sophisticated items of 'high' class bakery.

Milling

Since industrial roller technology was developed in the 1830s, most flour has been ground between high speed rollers. This generates heat from the friction of the rollers which alters some natural aspects of the flour, including the gluten level, the vitamins and enzymes and, arguably, the flavour. During the roller process, the bran and endosperm may be sifted out completely, leaving only fine particles of white flour.

The older method of grinding flour is between traditional millstones. Traditional stoneground whole-wheat flour does not have the bran and endosperm removed and therefore has a coarser texture, but more flavour since the germ contains oil giving it a higher food value than roller-milled white flour.

Bleaching

Unbleached white flours have a naturally creamy colour. They are left to age naturally, and this improves the flavour of the flour as well as the bread baked from it. Most mass produced flour is now treated with chemicals to make it whiter. This flour is bleached immediately after milling so it may be sold without the time-consuming period of natural ageing.

Types of flour

- **White flour** is ground finer and finer by repeated rolling. The extraction of the germ, with its oil content, means the keeping quality is improved. There are three basic types of plain flour: soft, hard and very hard (known as durum). The degree of hardness refers to the amount of gluten in the flour, soft having the least gluten and durum having the most. The Pekar Test is used to test gluten content. A bread dough is made, then a piece is washed in a sieve. The remainder, left in the sieve, establishes the gluten content. Bleached white flour may have been treated with chlorine gas. UK law stipulates that flour with an extraction rate of 80% or less must be enriched with B vitamins, and iron.

- **Plain fine cake flour** made from 100% soft wheat is the finest textured and is used for pastry, cakes and biscuits. It does not have raising agent added but has been selected from a fine grade of flour particles. However, some brands of plain flour have been specially selected from very fine flour particles which are also more even in size than other cheaper flours. They are particularly suitable for cakes, pastries etc. They may also be specially sifted. They are more expensive than regular plain flours, but worth it for a finer finished texture.

- **Strong plain flour**, made from more than 50% hard wheat, has the highest amount of gluten and is suitable for all breads since the gluten supports a strong open texture. Unbleached strong plain flour (white) or wholewheat will give the best tasting loaf. Wholewheat strong plain flour will not rise as well as white plain flour since it contains bran which inhibits the gluten.

- **Italian '00'** is a very finely milled flour used for pasta and pastries.

- **Standard self-raising flours** are made from plain flour to which baking powder (cream of tartar and bicarbonate of soda mixed with starchy filler) has been added. Long storage will diminish the power of the raising agent so check use-by date. Six-month-old will be less active than three-month old.

- **Special self-raising cake flours** are variously described as 'ideal for cakes and scones', 'light', 'supreme sponge', and 'extra fine'. What they all achieve is a higher rise and finer texture than standard self-raising flour. The main reason for their success in making a more tender crumb is that they have been selected from the finest grade of flour particles and are low in gluten (they may have been treated to reduce the gluten). They have a high starch content, and have usually been well sifted and aerated. This makes them much easier and quicker to sieve and mix than standard flours. Some claim they do not need to be sifted. They are more expensive but worth it for a finer finished texture.

Self-raising or plain?

Self-raising can be used for speed, but the use-by date must be checked. When using bicarbonate of soda with acid (lemon juice, buttermilk, sour cream, yougurt, treacle etc.) always use plain flour.

A fine-textured, soft plain flour suitable for cakes, rather than self-raising, is best when there is a high percentage of eggs, and the beating incorporates a lot of air, as in a Genoese or Dundee cake when a fine plain cake flour will always give a much finer texture.

- **Wholemeal** or **whole-wheat** flour is milled from the whole-wheat kernel including the bran and endosperm. It may be ground in the traditional way between millstones to make stone-ground flour which will produce a better flavour than roller ground. Grinding between slowly turning stones, powered by water or electricity, is becoming more common as the market increases for this old-fashioned type of wholemeal flour. In France there

are some 2500 independent small millers grinding this type of flour while in Britain, so far, only about 25. Wholemeal is a heavier, coarser flour which produces a heavier finished result but with the full nutrient value and flavour of the wheat grain.

- **Brown flour** is made with 80–90% of the bran and endosperm which makes it a lighter flour than wholemeal. The extraction rate should be shown on the packet. It usually contains most of the endosperm but will have had more of the bran removed than wholewheat flour.

- **Granary flour** is either wholemeal or brown flour with the addition of malted wheat and barley flakes.

Other flours

- **Barley flour**: A brownish/greyish flour with an earthy tang which may be made from traditional pearl barley or from the ancient Neolithic bere (barley), still grown in the North of Scotland and on Orkney. It is a low gluten flour so does not make a good rising bread but because of its good flavour it is used with other flours to add character to bread doughs. In the North of Scotland it is made into a girdle bannock with raising agent.

- **Buckwheat**: A dark earthy flour made from ground buckwheat which is indigenous to north-eastern Europe. A small proportion can be added to give added character to bread doughs.

- **Chestnut**: A light brown, nutty flavoured flour which is made from ground chestnuts.

- **Cornflour**: A fine white powdery flour with nil gluten which is made from the heart of the maize kernel.

- **Polenta**: A yellow cornmeal flour made from ground maize available in fine and rough textures. Used in Italy to make polenta and in the US to make cornbreads.

- **Potato**: A fine, white, soft, tasteless, low gluten flour which is made from pure potato starch. Used for thickening in delicately flavoured puddings and sauces.

• **Rice flour**: A fine, white flour which is made from white polished rice. Used in gluten-free cakes.

• **Rye**: A dark, low-gluten, tangy flavoured flour. It is used with a white wheat flour in sour-bread doughs. Fine rye is used in traditional Eastern European 'black' breads. Rough rye is used for coarse textured Pumpernickel.

FAT

In all baking the flavour of the fat has a vital influence on the finished result. While oil, white vegetable fat, lard and margarine may all be used, the most attractive fat flavour in sweet cakes, pastries and biscuits is butter. It is made by churning cream until it forms a solid mass when the fat globules are forced together. To remove the liquid droplets which are trapped among it the butter is then 'washed' leaving the butter with a fat content of around 80%.

• **Butter** taste depends on the method of production. Cultured butter is made from cream left to 'ripen' or sour naturally, or by adding a lactic culture. The end result is butter with a stronger flavour. Sometimes described as 'cheesy' butter, it is unlike most of UK butter, which is made from pasteurised cream. Most continental butter is cultured or ripened butter. This means that many of the enzymes and bacteria, which give it flavour, are not destroyed. Desirable flavours develop as the lactose (milk sugar) converts into lactic acid which provides the environment for the development of diacetyl, a potent fragrance, and the ingredient which gives this butter its distinctive taste.

Uncultured butter made from pasteurised cream has the enzymes and bacteria destroyed which means an inevitable flattening of flavour. The use of cultured butter in continental baking often explains its superior flavour.

The feed and breed of the cow also influences the butter taste so that where there is a wide variety of plants in the cow's diet, there will be a more interesting flavour in the butter. Butter from Jersey and Guernsey cows is a deeper yellow and richer flavour.

Butter taste also varies from spring through to winter with the best butter tastes to be found in spring and summer.

Most cultured butters are only lightly salted or unsalted, while most UK uncultured butters are salted, some quite heavily. The percentage of salt should be indicated on the label.

Unsalted butter is particularly good for baking since it has a sweet nutty flavour and a smooth firm texture. For most sweet baking it is important to use either an unsalted or a very lightly salted butter. Strongly salted butters may spoil the finished result, by making it too salty.

Cultured butters are less available and more expensive than regular uncultured UK butters. They should, therefore, only be used in baking where a special butteryness is vital to the finished result, in shortbread, for example.

• **Margarine** which is a blend of vegetable oils, milk and animal fats is the main butter alternative. Although it will never produce the same flavour as butter it can be used as a substitute, provided block margarine is used and not soft-tub margarine which has too high a water content. The same applies to low-fat margarines which have an even higher water content.

• **White cooking fats** are whipped from vegetable oils or a mix of vegetable oils and animal fats or fish oils. They are totally flavourless but are useful in baking since they give light results in cakes and tighten up the texture, if there are added ingredients which might otherwise sink to the bottom of a cake. They also 'shorten' pastries and biscuits, making them more crumbly. They are often used in conjunction with butter.

• **Lard** is a clear, hard fat made from rendered pork fat and was once used for all pastry making. It is still used in raised hot water pastry for traditional pork pies but white cooking fat is now used more frequently in other recipes.

- **Olive oil** is not used in sweet baking though extra virgin may be used in some traditional breads such as ciabatta.

SUGAR

This comes either from sugar cane, which grows in the tropics and sub-tropics, or sugar beet which grows in temperate regions.

The sugar refining process begins with unrefined molasses sugar which is a fine-grained, dark mixture with the texture of damp sand and a complex flavour. The process ends with one-dimensional flavoured powdery white icing sugar.

- **Granulated white sugar** is refined from cane or beet and is the most commonly used sugar, consisting of 100% pure sucrose. It is too coarse for cakes and pastries since it produces a speckled appearance.

- **Caster sugar** is finer than granulated and dissolves more easily. It is most often used in baking.

- **Icing sugar** is the finest consisting of 100% pure sucrose. Usually used for icings or for sifting over puddings and cakes. It is not used for cake-making since it does not create enough volume when creamed.

- **Brown sugars** may be made in two ways. Either from highly processed white beet sugar, which has had all its trace elements removed (this is then mixed with a small proportion of cane molasses to colour it brown) or they can be made by halting the refining process in which case they are 'unrefined' and may say so on the label. Unrefined will have a better flavour.

- **Molasses sugar** is dark, soft, fine-grained and damp with a strong flavour of treacle.

- **Dark Muscovado sugar** is one notch down: an unrefined, less intense sugar than molasses but still with a strong treacle flavour. (Muscovado is Portuguese for unrefined)

- **Light Muscovado sugar** is another notch down with the treacle flavour much lighter.

- **Demerara sugar** is a larger, coarser crystal than granulated with only a slight treacle flavour.

- **Light** and **Dark Soft Brown sugars** are usually refined white sugars which have been tossed in molasses or syrup.

- **Black treacle** is a more refined form of pure cane Molasses.

- **Vanilla Sugar** lends flavour to cakes and pastries. Instead of buying sugar which has been flavoured with vanilla extract, keep a vanilla pod in a jar of caster sugar and shake occasionally. The sugar will be infused with vanilla flavour in about two weeks.

- **Rock Sugar** is large crystals of cane sugar which is used for coffee but can also be used as decoration on biscuits and cakes.

Flavour and nutrient value:

'Unrefined' brown sugars usually come from ex-colonial countries such as Mauritius, Barbados and Guyana where entire communities depend on the sugar industry (both the growing and refining process) for jobs. These sugars have a better, fudgier flavour and produce a more interesting end result. They also contain more trace elements and vitamins, which occur naturally in sugar cane, but are normally lost by refining. They are now available in various grades from 'golden' (equivalent to white granulated but a golden colour); to 'soft brown' which is akin to caster sugar.

HONEY

While all honey is made by bees, the flavour, texture and viscosity depends on a number of variables. The most important of which is the flower the bee collects from.

- **Single blossom** or **'virgin' honey** is the most expensive but it also has the best flavour. Distinctively flavoured honeys include lavender, orange blossom, clover and rhododendron. It should be clear on the label that it is a single producer's 'virgin' (untampered) honey or an industrial producer's 'blended' mix. The difference is similar to an estate bottled extra virgin olive oil versus a commercially blended and processed oil from a variety of sources.

- **Scottish heather honey** comes from bees which have been taken to the heather clad hills during the summer months which gives the honey its strongly aromatic, slightly bitter flavour and dark colour.

- **Blended honeys** make up 83% of the UK market and usually have less defined flavours than virigin honey. Some may contain amounts of ordinary sugar. They may have a sickly sweet taste.

Charateristics and nutritional value

Viscosity varies according to the amount of water in the honey. Honey which has too much water – when it is very thin and runny – will also be lacking in flavour. Of the heather honeys, pure ling is the only one which is thixotropic, i.e. it is so thick it sets like a jelly. There are three major components of honey: fructose (38%), glucose (31%) and water (17%). The remaining 14% contains small amounts of some 22 ingredients including minerals, vitamins and enzymes. Compared with sugar, honey contains extra ingredients (traces of minerals, iron, calcium, magnesium, phosphorous, vitamins C, B, B2, B5, B6, nicotinic acid and other residues including enzymes, gums and resins) some of which will be destroyed if the honey is heated above 50 degrees C. There are also a number of rare sugars in honey, not normally found in nature, whose nutritional value remains, as yet, unexplored. Nutrients such as vitamin C and flavinoids (substances thought to increase effectiveness of vitamin C as an antioxidant in the body) have been found in honey, in small amounts. This varies in different honeys with the darkest having the highest antioxidant content.

Storing

Honey does not deteriorate if stored for 1–2 years at around room temperature. It does not like the cold and must be kept away from strong smells. Honey that has crystallised and set should be put in a bowl of warm water (not hotter than 50 degrees C) to melt.

EGGS

Quality will depend on method of production and feeding. Also on age.

Test for freshness

A fresh egg cracked onto a plate will have two layers of white, one thick and one thin with a 'proud' yolk which holds its shape. In time, the proteins in the white break down and the white becomes thin and watery. An old egg cracked onto a plate will have no thick white and will spread, the yolk floating in the white rather than being held in it.

Egg safety

Eggs are susceptible to salmonella since their shells are porous and can absorb bacteria. Thorough cooking will destroy salmonella but raw or lightly cooked eggs are used in many classic recipes. The risk is regarded as very small, but those at high risk – the elderly, the very young, pregnant women and those with an immune deficiency disease – should not eat raw or lightly cooked eggs.

Baking with eggs

Their unique culinary properties include the ability to bind a mixture, to thicken a sauce, to add richness and to create volume. To get the best out of them, they should always be at room temperature before use. When they are used as the raising agent in cakes they can be heated, to increase their volume when beaten, by putting the eggs in their shells in a bowl of very hot, but not boiling, water. They are then left for two minutes to heat the eggs through without cooking. Egg whites will only reach their full volume if they are whisked in a completely grease-free bowl. Glass, stainless steel or copper are preferable since plastic tends to hold grease. If using a plastic bowl, rinse with boiling water and salt using a paper towel to dry.

Whipped egg whites lose volume quickly so should only be beaten just before use. A pinch of salt breaks down the albumin and allows more air to be incorporated. Egg yolks should always be beaten before adding to sugar. They are more liable to curdle in a cake mixture if they are too cold.

YEAST

This is used in baking as a raising agent. It is a single-celled, living organism which produces carbon dioxide when it divides and multiplies. Conditions for successful fermentation include warmth, moisture and food. To trap the bubbles of carbon dioxide, the flour used in the dough must be 'strong' i.e. have a high gluten content giving it elastic qualities which will hold up the dough over the long fermenting period.

For centuries, traditional bread bakers used a slow-fermentation process allowing the yeast to ferment naturally. (When James Burgess began his apprenticeship in Drymen in the 1950s the daily bread was fermented for 14 hours.)

But in 1961, a new method was perfected known as the Chorleywood Bread Process (CBP) (*see* Baking a Better Loaf p.11). In large industrial 'plant' bakeries, this replaced the initial kneading of the dough as well as the long, 'first rise' slow-fermentation period. CBP introduced a short period of intense mechanicial dough development using a high-speed mixer. To get the dough to rise faster, the quantity of yeast was increased. Also a higher percentage of water was used making the lightweight, wrapped and sliced bread made in 'plant' bakeries today.

- **Wild yeast** is the natural microscopic yeast which is in air and from which bread has been made for at least 6000 years. It is usually caught in a 'starter' also known as a 'barm ferment' or 'poolish' which

is left to ferment naturally. This can be made from potatoes or grapes. It is then used to raise the dough. Subsequently a piece of the dough is kept back at each baking for raising the next dough. Sourdough breads made with wild yeast get their acid/sour flavour from the slow fermentation of the wild yeast and include German rye bread, Italian pagnotta and French pain au levain.

- **Fresh baker's yeast** is a by-product of the brewing industry and raises dough faster than wild yeast producing a sweeter, less tangy, lighter bread. It is a creamy beige, soft-solid consistency and should have a clean, sweet smell and break apart cleanly without crumbling. It can be kept in the fridge for up to a fortnight. It is usually blended with tepid liquid and some flour and left in a warm place for 20 minutes till it begins to froth. In professional baking this is known as a 'sponge dough process'.

- **Fast-action dried yeast** is powdered yeast that is very simple to use and can be added to the other ingredients without prior blending in liquid. It produces a bread with a less 'yeasty' aroma. Its use-by date should always be checked.

- **Dried yeast** has a larger grain than fast-action and must be blended with tepid water, a pinch of sugar and some flour before use. It should then be left for 20 minutes to check its freshness. If it does not froth up it should not be used. Its use-by date should always be checked.

- **Quantities to use**: 7g (¼ oz) fast action yeast is equivalent to 15g (½ oz) fresh yeast and 15ml (1 tablespoon) dried yeast.

OTHER RAISING AGENTS

- **Baking powder** is a mixture of bicarbonate of soda (alkali) and cream of tartar (acid) in a starchy filler base which releases carbon dioxide when mixed with liquid. Most commercial baking powders have a 'double-action' factor which means that only a fraction of the gas is released on contact with moisture. This means that it is not until heat is applied, when the item goes into the oven, that most of the carbon dioxide is released.

- **Bicarbonate of soda** is an alkali which reacts with acid to form carbon dioxide. The acid may be in the form of cream of tartar (1 part bicarbonte to 2 parts c of t). It may also be used on its own with acid agents such as buttermilk, lemon and treacle but only in items with a strong flavour since bicarbonate has an unpleasant taste on its own.

CHOCOLATE

Chocolate is made from the roasted and ground kernel of the cacao bean. It contains a complex mix of aromas and tastes depending on hundreds of different chemical compounds and including caffeine-like substances and stimulants such as theobromine and methyl-xanthine. Quality and character depend on the variety of the cacao bean, where and how it has been grown, as well as on the method of making the chocolate.

Cacao beans contain a high percentage of cocoa butter which is used widely in the cosmetic industry. Some British chocolate manufacturers sell the cocoa butter to the cosmetic industry and replace it in their chocolate with vegetable fat. That prompted other European chocolate makers to take them to the EU court claiming they could not call their product chocolate. The British, however, won their case.

Sweet milk chocolate, cheap 'cooking chocolate' and 'cake covering' chocolate, which have a low cocoa solid content (and possibly vegetable fat instead of cocoa butter), will not produce the best chocolate qualities in the finished result.

- **Plain dark chocolate** is made from cocoa solids which may vary in quantity from as little as 30% up to 99%. The rest of the chocolate consists of sugar and lecithin with vanilla flavouring. Its quality, however, is not to be judged on the percentage of its cocoa solids but on the quality of the original bean and the method of chocolate manufacture. The average percentage of cocoa solids is around 65-75%. Vanilla flavouring may come from the natural vanilla pod or from artificial 'vanillin' which produces a synthetic aftertaste. The best dark chocolate is said to come from France and Belgium, the best milk chocolate from Switzerland.

- **Couverture** is fine quality plain chocolate which is used by professional bakers and confectioners. It contains a high percentage of cocoa butter which requires tempering to achieve a high gloss finish. This is a complicated process involving heating and cooling to encourage the fat particles to form crystals which create the high gloss. If using, check the wrapper, which indicates what temperature the couverture should be melted at

- **White chocolate** is a mix of cocoa butter, milk solids and sugar with vanilla flavouring. Content of cocoa butter can vary from 20% to 45%. The less the percentage of cocoa butter, the more the sugar and milk solids. Some white chocolate has a very sweet taste. The best white chocolate is said to come from Holland.

To melt chocolate

This should always be done gently. Either in a double boiler or in a bowl over a pan of simmering water. The chocolate should be broken up into small pieces and allowed to melt without stirring. If it gets too hot, or if steam gets into the chocolate, it will 'seize up' and harden. It may also be melted in the microwave on a low setting and checked regularly.

The other method, which does not involve heating the chocolate on its own, is to break it up into very small pieces in a food processor and add cream which has just come off the boil.

To store chocolate

Keep airtight since it absorbs external odours and flavourings. Use foil to wrap rather than cling-film. Keep in a cool place since it melts easily. Milk and white chocolate should not be kept longer than 1 year while dark chocolate can be kept for up 3 years if stored correctly.

SPICES

Most spice is imported from India (mostly pepper, cardamom, chillies, ginger, turmeric and cumin) followed by Indonesia (pepper, nutmeg, mace, cassia, ginger, cardamom, vanilla), Madagascar (vanilla, cloves) and Malaysia (pepper, ginger).

More than 80% of spices come from developing countries where production and export is an important element of their agricultural economy.

Differences in quality depend on climate, soil and how the crop has been grown, harvested and stored.

Oil content of ginger, cinnamon and cloves

Though ginger is grown throughout the spice world, Jamaican ginger is widely regarded as the best. It is also the most expensive. Grown in small quantities, it is the specially good growing conditions, plus the rich soils, which have increased the level of essential oil in their ginger giving it a deep yellow colour. Most is made into ginger oil and none is now sold as ground ginger in the UK. Other differences in quality depend on the methods of production, distribution and storing. Ginger can loose its pungency if it has been treated to remove some of its oils before grinding. Cinnamon and cloves are the other spices most likely to have had some oil extracted. It is surprising the difference in pungency between brands. Top spice buyers will laboratory-test spices before buying to check the oil content. They will also prefer to buy whole, rather than ground.

Storing

Exposure to light, warmth and air will also deplete spicy pungency. Ultra violet light dries out the oil and lightens the colour of the spice. Those sitting on shelves in clear glass jars for too long will eventually loose their potency. To test the quality of a spice, buyers judge first by the aroma. Then, if it's ground, they will put a pinch in the palm of the hand and rub gently with the thumb to release the full aroma.

Buying

The best, and cheapest, way to buy spices is from small companies. This is because they buy in small quantities and the spices are sold faster and will therefore be fresher. Buying from small mail order companies can provide a saving of 30-50% compared with the prices of the larger market leaders who have higher overheads and large advertising budgets to finance.

SALT

The type of salt used in baking may be important to the finished result, especially in breadmaking where salt plays an important part.

While all salt enhances and develops flavour, salt from seawater and rock salt which is mined, are the most intense. It is reckoned that because of their pungency, a third less sea or rock salt will be required to develop flavour than industrial salt.

Sea and rock salt contain many more minerals and do not have the bitter aftertaste of industrial salt which consists mainly of sodium choride plus starch to make it flow.

While rock salt is mined and then processed into flakes, salt from seawater involves a network of canals on flat coastal lands. In the last decade or so, sea salt from the marshes of Le Guerandais on the West Coast of France has been revived with a co-op set up in 1989. Sun and wind evaporate the water and the salt sinks to the botton. It may take on a greyish colour from the clay. This is the cheapest form of sea salt known as grey salt. More expensive is the Fleur de Sel. This comes from a thin crystalline layer which forms on top of the salt pans and which is scooped up before it sinks. It has the finest flavour.

Techniques and Tips

BREADS

All that bread wants is time and warmth, so the saying goes, as well as four ingredients: flour, water, yeast and salt. There is, of course, another vital ingredient which is your time and effort. This is sometimes in short supply, which is where the modern 'bread-maker' comes in, bringing a new dimension to baking a 'daily loaf'. And as the machine takes over the techniques – kneading, rising and baking – so it illustrates how simple and easy it is to make a loaf.

It does not, however, succeed in producing a loaf with an interesting shape or a crisp crust. Use the machine as kneader and prover only, shape the dough by hand and bake it in a conventional oven and you will get the best of both worlds.

A survey of home baking (*Bread Facts 2001*) maintained that 1 in 10 men bake bread at home, 53% from scratch 47% with a breadmaker. Many offices now have their own breadmaker, programming it to produce a loaf in time for lunch while filling the office with delectable yeasty aromas.

Personal breadmaking looks set for an interesting future as more books appear, making the compromise of kneading and rising in the breadmaker and shaping and baking by hand.

Kneading by hand

Kneading by hand gives the baker more control over the dough compared with the labour-saving breadmaker or the mechanical method used in commercial bakeries. The dough consistency is important to the finished result. It should be soft and slightly sticky. If it's too stiff, the texture will be too tight and the dough will not rise well. If it's too soft it will be a soggy texture.

Begin by folding the edges into the centre, pressing down with the heel of your palm each time. Keep rotating the dough about a quarter turn each time you fold a bit in. Once the dough begins to form a smooth ball continue pressing out with one hand folding in, turning a quarter and pressing out again. The texture of the dough will begin to change as the kneading develops the elastic nature of the gluten.

The change will be from a soft, stickyish consistency into a more solid smooth, springy ball of dough. If the dough texture is too stiff before kneading it will not change consistency in this way. Alternately, if it is too sticky before kneading, more flour will have to be added. Kneading by hand is a more sensitive way of achieving the correct consistency which will, inevitably, determine the success of the finished loaf. Kneading can also be done in an electric mixer with a dough hook which can work well providing you keep checking that the consistency is right.

Shaping the dough by hand

Shaping the dough by hand involves turning in all the edges to the centre, then turning the dough over so the smooth underside is uppermost.

Variations:

- **For a small round bun or roll**, dust the work surface and, holding the dough under the palm of your hand, rotate it, tucking the edges of the dough under with the ends of your fingers. This compacts the dough and helps the strands of gluten to align, which is what makes the bread/roll rise in a good round shape during baking. Use only enough flour to prevent sticking.

- **For a round cob loaf**, tuck the edges in all the way round, turn over so the underside is uppermost and – holding the dough in your two palms – drag and turn the ball firmly across the work surface. As with the rolls/buns, this compacts the dough and strengthens the gluten ensuring a better shaped finished loaf.

- **Shaping for a traditional tin loaf**, flatten the dough into an oblong, the length of the tin but three times wider. Fold in three, then place in the tin. It should come no more than two-thirds up the tin.

- **Shaping for a cottage loaf**, cut off one third of the dough and shape both pieces as for a cob loaf. Wet the edges of the larger piece and place smaller piece on top. Then take the handle of a wooden spoon and press down through the middle to make the traditional dent.

- **Shaping a plait**, divide the dough into three and shape each piece into a long roll. Pinch the ends together and plait, loosely tucking both ends under.

- **Slashing the top of the dough** allows the dough to expand and open out when baked. It should only be done with a razor sharp knife. Some bakers use a razor blade. A blunt knife will tear the dough and damage the shape. Slashes may be simple diagonal cuts across the dough or a cross cut on a round loaf or a diamond pattern.

- **For a crisp crust** wash the bread periodically with water during the baking.

Some common failures in breadmaking:

- **Dough does not rise or rises very slowly**: the yeast is stale. Or the liquid was too hot and killed the yeast. Or the dough was left to rise in a place which was too hot. Avoid rising doughs in stainless steel bowls which can get too hot and kill the yeast.

- **Loaf collapses in the oven**: dough was left too long in the second rising and became over-risen which over-stretched the gluten. It should rise to double its size and no more.

- **Bread is soggy, damp and dense**: too much liquid was added or the dough was not kneaded long enough to develop the gluten. It may also have been baked too slowly or taken out of the oven before it was thoroughly baked through.

- **Crust rises unevenly**: uneven heat in the oven. Turn the loaves half way through the baking.

- **Free-form shaped rolls and breads spread** during baking: the dough was too soft when shaped.

- **Bread stales very quickly**: too much yeast was used in the dough. Or the dough was risen too rapidly.

PASTRIES

The secret of successful pastries depends on accurate measuring, the correct proportions of fat to flour, and keeping cool. This means keeping everything cool: kitchen, work surface (marble is the best surface for pastry) ingredients, and your hands.

- **'Resting' pastry** in the fridge between rollings and shapings is also important since it gives it time to cool down. It also gives the gluten time to 'relax' making it easier to roll out again. Pastry which has not been rested will be difficult to roll out and will also shrink when baked.

- **Flour used for pastry** should preferably be a fine plain flour. Self-raising flour is not suitable since it gives a spongy pastry while wholemeal tends to give a very heavy pastry unless it is used only as a small percentage of the total flour content. French pastry flour is expensive but it gives excellent results. Most French bakers working in the UK import French flour since it is not widely available. Italian '00', which is similar to the French pastry flour, is specially recommended for pastry and is now widely available.

- **Fats used for pastry making** are a matter of taste, though all butter will give the best flavour. Pastry is traditionally made with a mixture of lard or white vegetable fat (this is for extra shortness) and butter or margarine. If margarine is used it should be a hard block margarine rather than a soft spreading variety which contains too much water. The same applies to soft spreading butter which, similarly, has too much water. Fats should be unsalted or lightly salted. Some butters are very highly salted and may make the end result too salty.

- **Adding the fats to the flour** can be done by hand – rubbing the fat into the flour with your fingertips. Cut the fat into small pieces first and then pick up small amounts at a time, rubbing it through your fingers to break it down into small pieces. It should be done as lightly as possible until the mixture resembles fine breadcrumbs. This can also be done in the food processor.

- **Water should be cold** when added to pastry and should be added with care. Too much will make the pastry too hard, while too little will make it too crumbly. The liquid should be sprinkled evenly over the surface. A round-bladed knife should be used to mix in. It is better not to add all the liquid at once since flours vary in their absorption qualities with some taking more water and some less. Once the dough begins to come together, collect it in a ball and knead for a few seconds until it is smooth. Iced water is best for Danish pastries and Puff pastry.

- **Making pastry in the blender** is the alternative method, the flour and fats (cut up into small pieces) can be put into the blender and pulsed until they resemble fine breadcrumbs. To ensure the pastry is not overworked use the pulse button in short bursts, checking the consistency regularly. Add the liquid one tablespoon at a time. It is best to make pastry in small quantities in the blender since it is easier to control the consistency if the bowl is not too full.

- **Ready-made pastry** is now widely available and is useful if time is limited. Ready-made puff pastry is particularly useful since this is one of the more complicated and time-consuming pastries. Other pastries, such as shortcrust, are quick and easy to make in the blender and much cheaper than the

ready-made alternative. As a rough guide, a 375g (13oz) packet of shortcrust pastry is roughly equivalent to homemade pastry made with 250g (8oz) flour. Approximately 750g (1lb 10oz) puff pastry is equivalent to homemade puff made with 450g (1lb) flour.

- **Rolling out pastry** should be done on a cool, floured work surface. Roll in light firm strokes, turning the pastry frequently to give an even shape and thickness. Avoid pulling or stretching the pastry while rolling, since it will be liable to shrink during cooking if it has been overstretched. A soft 'table' brush, (used for clearing crumbs) or other similar soft brush is a useful tool for brushing off excess flour as you work. In professional baking this process is known as keeping the pastry 'green'.

- **Baking 'blind'** is when the pastry is part cooked before a filling is added. This involves placing a sheet of foil or greaseproof paper in the base of the flan or pastry case, then filling it with something which will hold it down gently, such as dried pulses, rice or dried bread crusts. This prevents the base of the pastry rising when trapped air underneath it expands on heating causing bubbles.

  If a non-liquid filling is being used, such as jam, it is not necessary to use the paper and beans method, but the base can be pricked all over with a fork which will also prevent it from rising. If a liquid filling is being used, such as a quiche, the base and sides should be painted with a beaten egg and returned to the oven to make a 'seal' which will prevent the filling making the pastry soggy.

CAKES

The secret of successful cake baking depends on getting the correct balance of strengthening and tenderising ingredients in the cake mix.

This means that the flour and eggs – which contain the proteins and strengthen the cake – should be perfectly balanced with the sugar, butter and liquids which soften and tenderise it.

If the proportion of flour and eggs is too high, the cake texture will be too dry, tough and hard. If, on the other hand, they are too low, the cake will not hold its shape, collapsing in the oven or as it cools.

Because this balance is easily disturbed, it is important in cake making to follow recipes precisely.

- **Cake ingredients should be at room temperature**, butter and eggs lukewarm. Neither should be used straight from the fridge. Butter should be soft, but not runny. Eggs should be warmed by putting them, still in their shells, into a bowl of very hot, but not boiling, water where they should be left for 2 minutes to warm through without cooking.

- **Fats used** will determine the final character of the cake. Butter will give the best flavour to cakes. Margarine will not give such a good flavour, but if it is used it should be a hard block margarine rather than a soft spreading variety which has too high a water content. The same applies to soft spreading butter which also has too much water added. White vegetable fats may be used for their ability to tighten the structure of the cake and prevent added ingredients, such as fruit and nuts, sinking.

- **Mixing** may be done by hand, with a balloon whisk, or with an electric mixer. It is important to preserve the cake's airy structure especially for egg-based cakes which depend on the delicate egg foam structure for their success. Flour and other ingredients should always be folded in very gently with a large metal spoon using a cutting and folding technique in a figure of eight movement.

- **Lining tins** with silicone, greaseproof or foil provides protection for the cake. Always grease with oil and dust with flour rather than use butter or margarine which tend to make the mixture stick. For a very large fruit cake it is advisable to place a strip, several layers thick, of brown paper round the outside of the tin and tie it with string to give more protection during the long baking time.

- **Baking the cake**: If success is to be achieved once it is in the oven, the temptation to open the door too soon must be resisted. A sudden rush of cold air, if it has not set sufficiently, may make it sink in the middle. It is best to wait for at least 30 minutes before opening the oven door. If it appears to be browning too quickly, cover with a sheet of foil towards the end of the cooking. If it is browning unevenly, turn the cake tin in the oven.

- **To test a sponge**, remove from the oven and test by touching gently in the centre when it should spring back.

- **To test a large fruit cake**, take it out of the oven and insert a skewer into the centre. It should come out clean – if any of the mixture is still sticking, return the cake to the oven and bake for a little longer, then check again. All cakes are best left in their tins to cool and set a little, before turning out of their tins.

- **Serving cakes and pastries with wine** at the end of the meal, or at other times of the day, requires some thought towards matching suitable tastes and flavours. The best wines to serve are the naturally sweet dessert wines such as the Sauternes and Muscats. These wines are served well chilled. Cakes and pastries should always be less sweet than the wines served with them otherwise the subtlety of the wine will be lost. Flavourings, such as chocolate, are difficult to match with wine though more robust flavours such as Ruby Port or a Cognac can work.

- **Storing cakes** successfully depends on their richness. The richer the cake the better it will store. Rich fruit cakes and gingerbreads actually improve with keeping. Wrap in clingfilm or greaseproof paper and foil. Do not use foil with a rich fruitcake since the fruit may react with it. Store in a cool dry place. If freezing sponges, it's best to do so before filling and decorating.

SCONES

The secret of a good scone depends largely on the consistency of the dough, which should be soft and elastic. The mixing should be done quickly and lightly. The best method, and the way professional bakers mix, is on the table, without a bowl. All the dry ingredients are sifted onto the work surface. Then a well is made in the middle for the liquid and a plastic scraper is used to bring the dough together. This ensures the minimum of mixing and handling of the soft dough. To get the outer crust crisp they should be baked in a very hot oven until they are just risen and dried out. The inside should be soft and fluffy.

- **Traditional Scottish (and Irish) scones** are made with buttermilk and bicarbonate of soda—known as Soda Scones. There is a subtle difference in the finished scone, which is softer, lighter, moister and with a tangy flavour compared with scones made with fresh milk, egg, sugar and baking powder. If buttermilk is not available then fresh milk can be soured by adding lemon juice.

- **Mixing and shaping** involves light quick handling for a perfect result. The flour should be well sifted and the buttermilk poured into a well in the centre. Don't add the liquid drop by drop. Stir with a fork, gradually bringing in the flour; if the mixture is too dry and 'ragged' looking, the scones will not be light. The mixing should be done with as little 'working' as possible and it should be a soft elastic consistency. It should be handled as little as possible and for this reason it is best lifted out of the bowl in well-floured hands and placed on either girdle or baking tray. Then it can be well floured on top and lightly pressed down into a rough round shape (a bannock) for the girdle ½ inch (1½ cm) and for the oven 1¼ inch (3½ cm). Only at this point is it divided into scones. If liked, they may either be cooked separate or touching. If they are not separated they will take longer to cook.

- **Baking** can be done either on a traditional girdle or in the oven. There will be differences in shape and texture. Those baked on the girdle will have smooth flat top and bottom surfaces while those from the oven will be rough on top. Oven scones are more likely to be drier while girdle scones will be moister.

- Girdle baking allows more control over the baking since you can watch them as they cook and learn to judge when they should be turned and, more importantly, when they are ready. The girdle should not be too hot at the start of the baking or the scones will brown too quickly. Bake till risen and there is a white skin on top. This usually takes about five or six minutes. The heat should have penetrated to the top, and the centre should be well set before turning. This is important, if the centre is not set it will go soggy on turning. Increase the heat if necessary to brown the underside then turn and brown on the other side. They should take about 15 minutes altogether. Open up a little at the edge to check they are quite dry inside. Wrap in a towel to keep them soft. It is more difficult to judge when they are cooked through in the oven but they will take a shorter time than you imagine. If overcooked or undercooked, they will lose their softness and lightness.

- **To season a girdle**: Rub some oil into the surface and put on to heat. Allow to burn a skin on, leaving it till it smokes. Make a milk and flour pouring batter and pour onto the surface while hot. Leave it until it burns on one side then turn and burn on the other side. This should be done several times or until the surface is 'seasoned' i.e. the mixture no longer sticks and you have created a non-stick surface.

Equipment

Home bakers can now enjoy the benefits of labour saving equipment that was once only available to professional bakers. Beating and blending has become a question of turning on a switch, but there are still occasions when hand mixing is a better method. Folding flour into a delicate whisked egg sponge, for instance, is something which can only be done with a large metal spoon and a light touch.

Hand-held or free-standing mixer?

The hand-held mixer has the advantage of being more convenient to use since it allows you to control the movement around the bowl. While they are convenient and easy to use for short periods, they are less good for long periods of beating, or for large quantities of mixture. They are unsuitable for mixing yeast dough which should be done with the dough hook of a free-standing electric mixer in quantities up to 750g (1½ lb). Beware of using larger quantities in any electric mixer since it may burn out the motor.

Balloon Whisks

Particularly good for beating air into egg whites by hand since they produce a good, airy froth while electric mixers can produce a texture which is a little too dense. The handle of the whisk should have a good grip.

Food Blenders

Useful in baking for mixing flour and butter (instead of rubbing in), and for making pastry and biscuits. They are also helpful in chopping ingredients such as fruit and nuts though if pulsed for too long the texture will be lost. Hand-held blenders are useful for blending small quantities in the bowl, though are time-consuming if the quantity is large.

Breadmaking machines

Useful for home-bakers who do not want to get involved in mixing and kneading a dough. They depend on a mixing/baking unit and a computer control panel which allows regulation of timings, mixings, provings and bakings. While they are useful for bakers who want everything done for them, they are also versatile enough to be used only for mixing and proving when the dough can then be removed and moulded and baked in the conventional oven. They are limited in the shape of the finished baked bread and also in the amount of dough they will bake, the largest up to 900g (2lb).

Cake tins and baking trays or sheets

These should be a convenient size for your oven and made of the thickest gauge of metal you can afford. The thicker the gauge, the less likely they are to warp or develop hot spots.

- **Heavy-gauge anodised aluminium** is particularly good for baking trays.

- **Tin** is a common metal for baking tins since it heats up quickly but it also rusts easily so must be washed and dried thoroughly.

- **Non-stick tins** are useful though their surfaces can get scratched easily.

- **Spring-release** (also known as springform) cake tins are useful for delicate cakes and cheesecakes which you would not want to invert to turn out.

- **Metal flan tins** with removable bases are better for tarts, pies and quiches than ceramic dishes which do not conduct the heat very well and can make pastry go soggy.

Lining papers

These come in a variety of types and are essential with most cakes to prevent sticking, making them easier to unmould.

- **Greaseproof paper** has a waterproof coating and is useful for lining tins as well as wrapping cakes and biscuits for storage

- **Silicone paper** is both heat and grease-resistant and is more durable than greaseproof, it should last indefinitely. It is more expensive but worth it.

- **Non-stick baking parchment** is very strong, stiff paper which is heat and grease-resistant.

- **Silicone sheet 'Silpat'** (cannot be cut) is a thick non-stick mat which needs no greasing. It is useful for delicate items since the thickness prevents over-browning on the base. Expensive but worth it.

- **Rice paper** (edible) is useful for lining cakes and meringues which stick easily. It need not be removed once the item is cooked.

Ovens

Possibly the most important piece of equipment the baker will use, so knowing your oven is vital to baking success. Though all ovens are fitted with thermostats they are not always accurate and it is sometimes necessary to make slight adjustments according to your own experience. Some modern ovens are fan-assisted which means they have constantly circulating air which avoids hot and cold spots in the oven. They may bake in a shorter time than in the conventional oven. Convection ovens which have been incorporated into dual microwaves have revolving turntables which provide the most even heat.

In a non-fan oven, the hottest part is at the top where the hot air rises, and the coolest part at the bottom. It is best to use the middle shelves and, unless the oven is fan-assisted, turn the trays round half way through the cooking. Also make sure that items are spaced a few inches in from the edge of the baking tray to avoid browning too much at the edges. It is also best not to overload the oven, especially for items which need a crisp result such as biscuits and pastry, since a too full oven will produce too much moisture.

Measuring

Electronic scales

The most up-to-date system with such sophistications as add-and-weigh functions. This allows resetting the display or dial to zero once you have weighed an item so you can weigh other ingredients on top. Digital displays can usually be switched from metric to imperial instantly. Some have a memory function.

Spring-operated scales

Use the tension stored in the spring to balance against the ingredients. They are usually limited in the weight they can hold. This depends on the strength of the spring.

Balance scales

These depend on weights set on one tray against the ingredients to be weighed on the other. They work on the see-saw principle with the ingredient weight achieved when the two balance. They are the simplest and oldest method of weighing.

Measuring spoons

Fast and convenient measures. Spoons usually come joined together and range from 1.25ml (¼ tsp) up to 15ml (1 tablespoon). Cups are widely used in America and Australia.

Standard measuring spoons

These are the same as the metric measuring spoons now widely available in Britain.
All spoon measures are taken as level.

For Liquids:

¼ teaspoon = 1.25ml
½ teaspoon = 2.5ml
1 teaspoon = 5 ml
1 tablespoon = 15 ml (3 teaspoons)
2 tablespoons = 30ml
5 tablespoons = 75ml
8 tablespoons = 120ml

Measuring cups

A quick and easy way of measuring, small quantities. With large quantities they become too time-consuming. Those available are based on the American cup weighing system based on the old British measure of 1 pint = 16 fl oz which was abandoned in 1825. (1 UK pint is now = 20 fl oz.)

Graduated in fractions of 1 cup (8fl oz) there are usually five sizes in the set—

⅛ cup = 1 fl oz (30ml)
¼ cup = 2fl oz (60ml)
⅓ cup = 2½ fl oz (80ml)
½ cup = 4fl oz (125ml)
1 cup = 8fl oz (250ml approx.)

Imperial to Metric

While baking often requires exactness, weighing for everyday cooking does not need the same kind of precision. Half an ounce, here and there, will not ruin the recipe. And in any case, basic items like flour, sugar, butter and margarine also vary in moisture content. Final results can also be influenced by the weather – hot, wet, dry, and cold – as well as by the temperature of the kitchen.

Scales and measures are usually graduated in multiples of 25g. If the conversion of 1oz to 25g is made (1oz = 28.35g) therefore it's inevitable that there will be inaccurate jumps, e.g. when you move from 3 to 4oz. Should you use $3\frac{1}{2}$oz for 100g or 4oz? Should you use 4oz for 125g or $4\frac{1}{2}$oz which is a more exact conversion?

The answer is that where it might alter the balance of the recipe and cause failure i.e. in cakes, the exact conversion has been chosen, although it may be less convenient to measure.

Easier and faster measuring, when converting to metric in small quantities for domestic baking, is the system which compares quantities proportionately since all ingredients are now sold and packaged in metric:

4oz = 125g , 8oz = 250g , 16oz = 500g

For liquid measurements, following the American cup measures, the same proportional system would mean:

4fl oz = 125ml, 8fl oz = 250ml , 16fl oz = 500ml

The disadvantage of this method is that when moving up into larger quantities the differences become greater i.e. 1kg = (not 2lb) but 2lb 4oz

ALWAYS USE EITHER METRIC OR IMPERIAL – DO NOT MIX THE TWO.

Weight:
15g ($\frac{1}{2}$oz)
25g (1oz)
40g ($1\frac{1}{2}$oz)
50g (2oz approx. or $1\frac{3}{4}$ oz exact)
75g (3oz approx. or $2\frac{3}{4}$oz exact)
100g (4oz approx. or $3\frac{1}{2}$oz exact)
125g (4 oz approx. or $4\frac{1}{2}$ exact)
150g (5oz approx. or $5\frac{1}{2}$oz exact)
175g (6oz)
200g (7oz)
225g (8oz)
250g (8oz approx. or 9oz exact)
275g (9oz approx. or $9\frac{1}{2}$oz exact)
300g (10oz approx. or $10\frac{1}{2}$oz exact)
325g (11oz approx. or $11\frac{1}{2}$oz exact)
350g (12oz)
375g (13oz)
400g (14oz)
425g (15oz)
450g (16oz)
500g (16oz approx. or 1lb 2oz exact)
600g (1lb 5oz)
750g (1lb 10oz)
1kg (2lb approx. or 2lb 4oz exact)
2.25kg (5lb)

Volume:
15ml ($\frac{1}{2}$ fl oz)
25ml (1fl oz)
50ml (2fl oz)
75ml (3fl oz approx. or $2\frac{1}{2}$fl oz exact)
100ml (3fl oz approx. or $3\frac{1}{2}$fl oz exact)
125ml (4fl oz)
150ml (5fl oz, $\frac{1}{4}$pt)
175ml (6fl oz)
200ml (7fl oz, $\frac{1}{3}$pt)
250ml (8fl oz approx. or 9fl oz exact)
300ml (10 fl oz, $\frac{1}{2}$pt)
325ml (11fl oz)
350ml (12fl oz)
400ml (14fl oz)
425ml (15fl oz, $\frac{3}{4}$pt)
450ml (16fl oz)
475ml (17fl oz)
500ml (20fl oz approx. or 18fl oz exact)
600ml (20fl oz, 1pt)
1L (2pt approx. or $1\frac{3}{4}$ pt exact)
1.2L (2pt)
2L ($3\frac{1}{2}$pt)
3L ($5\frac{1}{4}$pt)

Sugar Thermometer

This is the most reliable way to check the temperature of boiling sugar syrup. Before use, check in boiling water to make sure it is working correctly. Alternative testing of boiling syrups, without a thermometer, can be done successfully by using the following tests:

A few drops of the boiling sugar dropped into a cup of cold water will tell you exactly what stage the sugar is at. Remove the pan from the heat while testing since a few minutes boiling can take the sugar to a higher temperature than is required result. If the result of the testing in water is a little past the desired stage, add a little warm water to lower the temperature and continue.

Stages in Sugar Boiling

- **Smooth/Transparent icing** (108°C) for crystallising purposes and fondant. The mixture begins to look syrupy. To test, dip finger in water and then very quickly into the syrup, the thumb will slide smoothly over the fingers, but the sugar will cling.

- **Softball** (115°C) for soft caramel, candy, fudge and tablet. To test, drop a little syrup into cold water and leave for a few minutes. Pick up between the finger and thumb when it should roll into a small softball.

- **Firm or hard ball** (121°C) for caramels, marshmallows, nougat, Edinburgh Rock and soft toffee. Test as above – the syrup should roll into a hard ball.

- **Small crack** (138°C) for toffees and rock. Test as above, when the thread of syrup should break lightly.

- **Hard crack** (154°C) for hard toffees, boiled sweeties and drops, pulled sugar and rock. Test as above, when the thread of syrup should break sharply.

- **Caramel** (160°C upwards). When the syrup begins to discolour, turning a darker brown colour, caramel stage is reached. If allowed to become too dark, the taste will be bitter.

Early Morning Yeast Baking

No other item of Western food culture is as basic as our daily bread. 'Give us this day ...' we ask. And when the house fills with warming aromas of yeast baking, there is the comforting thought of a slice of good bread with the next meal.

Will it be a crisp, burnished brown, caramelised crust enclosing a soft, white, springy interior?

Whatever the style, it is sure to have the unique character of something which has been sensitively hand-crafted. It may not be as perfect as its shop bought alternative. It may have cost time and effort in the making. But its rewards, for both eaters and bakers, can only be measured in the enjoyment of its taste and texture.

'Manna' is bread, the gift of life. Eat bread and have a long and healthy life.

DOS AND DON'TS

'If at first you don't succeed, don't give up. I studied yeast for nearly ten years at night school and baked with it nearly every day of my working life. It's an art in itself and I'm always learning.'

• Do not mix yeast and salt and spices together: they will kill the yeast.

• If you have a dough with a lot of spice, add extra yeast.

• Fermentation likes a warm atmosphere. Keep the kitchen warm and without draughts.

• Tepid water is hand, or lukewarm.

• Do not use too much flour when rolling up. Just a slight dust.

• If using fresh yeast, use baker's yeast and keep covered in a plastic tub in the fridge, not in the freezer.

• Use oil to grease trays rather than fat which burns the base of the bread or rolls.

• Cover your fermentation at all times with a damp tea towel or lightly oiled clingfilm, leaving uncovered puts a skin on the dough and prevents it rising so well. If not covered, when baked, your dough may be patchy and cracked on top.

• Some bread flours take more water than others so you may have to adjust the liquid required accordingly.

• The faster you bake a properly fermented roll or bun, the better it will taste.

• Dust baking trays with semolina to give a crunchy base to rolls and buns.

• Do not prove bread or rolls near a naked flame. The dough will be overactivated and the result will be small in size.

• The bread in these recipes was made in my home kitchen without steam.

YEAST

Baker's yeast – quick-action, fresh or dried – how much to use?

Yeast necessary to raise 500g (1lb) flour in approximately 1 hour:

7g (¼ oz) quick-action yeast, or

15g (½ oz) fresh yeast, or

15ml (1 tablespoon) dried yeast.

The advantage of quick-action yeast is that it can be mixed directly in to the flour. Both fresh yeast and dried yeast must be mixed with liquid before they can be added.

To speed up the process you can add more yeast. Though this will reduce the keeping quality of the bread.

To kick-start the yeast into action you can mix it with some of the tepid liquid and add a few tablespoons of flour and leave it in a warm place until it begins to bubble and froth. This has two advantages: firstly it confirms that the yeast is alive and well (sometimes a problem with dried yeast and quick-action if it has been stored too long) and secondly it produces a more yeasty, better-keeping bread.

Daily bread *with fresh yeast*

'This was our One Devonshire *bread (1991-2001). It was made with fresh yeast throughout the day, according to demand, so it was always fresh. We made it in 3lb batches which were divided into small rolls, plaits and tin loaves.'*

Yield: 7–8 bread rolls and 2 x ½ kg (1lb) loaves

500g (1lb 2oz) strong white bread flour

1 teaspoon dried milk powder

I level teaspoon sea salt

2 level teaspoons caster sugar

40g (1½ oz) fresh yeast

300ml (10fl oz) tepid water

1½ tablespoons vegetable oil

1 large egg, beaten

1 egg beaten with 1 teaspoon water for glazing

Toppings:
sesame or poppy seeds, grated Parmesan cheese, chopped chives, flaked almonds

- Preheat the oven to 425°F/220°C/Gas 7. Grease 2 x ½ kg (1lb) loaf tins, baking trays for rolls. Electric mixer with dough hook OR knead by hand. For full description of hand-kneading method see p.29.

- KNEADING DOUGH IN ELECTRIC MIXER: Put flour, dried milk powder, salt and sugar into the bowl of electric mixer. Mix the yeast with a little of the tepid water to make a thin cream. Start the machine on slow using dough hook and add the oil and egg mixture first and then the creamed yeast and most of the water. Check the consistency. It should be soft but not too sticky. Add the rest of the water if too stiff. Knead for 5 minutes on a fast speed (knead 10 minutes by hand, see p.29). Remove and put into a greased bowl. Cover with a damp tea towel or lightly oiled clingfilm.

- PROVING: Leave in a warm (24-30°C/75-85°F), preferably humid place, out of draughts, but not near any naked heat, till doubled in size.

- SHAPING Knock down and knead till smooth. Shape into rolls, plaits or tin loaves. Put on baking tray. Cover loosely with lightly oiled clingfilm and put back in the same warm, humid place to rise again

- FINISHING: Glaze with beaten egg and top with sesame or poppy seeds, grated Parmesan cheese, chopped chives or flaked almonds.

- BAKING: Bake for 10–15 minutes until risen and browned for rolls – 30–40 minutes for ½ kg (1lb) tin loaves. Test for readiness: the base should sound hollow when tapped. Cool on rack. When completely cold wrap in clingfilm if storing.

Wholemeal loaves or rolls
with fresh yeast

'This mix uses half wholemeal and half strong white since 100% wholemeal would hold back the fermentation and make a very heavy loaf.'

Yield: 7–8 bread rolls and 2 x ½ kg (1lb) loaves

250g (9oz) wholemeal or granary flour

250g (9oz) strong white bread flour

1 teaspoon dried milk powder

I level teaspoon sea salt

2 level teaspoons sugar

40g (1½ oz) fresh yeast

300ml (10fl oz) tepid water

1½ tablespoons vegetable oil

1 large egg, beaten

1 tablespoon black treacle

1 egg beaten with 1 teaspoon water for glazing

Toppings:
toasted coarse oatmeal, rolled oats, dusting of granary flour sesame or poppy seeds

- Preheat the oven to 425°F/220°C/Gas 7. Grease 2 x ½ kg (1lb) loaf tins, baking trays for rolls Electric mixer with dough hook OR knead by hand. For full description of hand-kneading method see p.29.

- KNEADING DOUGH IN ELECTRIC MIXER: Put the two flours, dried milk powder, salt and sugar into the bowl of electric mixer. Mix the yeast with a little of the tepid water to a thin cream. Using dough hook, start the machine on slow and add the oil and egg beaten with the treacle mixture first and then the creamed yeast and most of the water. Check the consistency. It should be soft but not too sticky. Add the rest of the water if too stiff. Knead for 5 minutes on a fast speed (knead 10 minutes by hand, see p.29). Remove and put into a greased bowl. Cover with a damp tea towel or lightly oiled clingfilm.

- PROVING: Leave in a warm (24-30°C/75-85°F), preferably humid place, out of draughts, but not near any naked heat, till doubled in size.

- SHAPING: Knock down and knead till smooth. Shape into rolls, plaits or tin loaves. Put on baking tray. Cover loosely with lightly oiled clingfilm and put back in the same warm, humid place to rise again.

- FINISHING: Brush with beaten egg and top with sesame or grated parmesan or flaked almonds.

- BAKING: Bake for 10–15 minutes until risen and browned for rolls – 30–40 minutes for ½ kg (1lb) tin loaves. Test for readiness: the base should sound hollow when tapped. Cool on rack. When completely cold wrap in clingfilm if storing.

Quick white loaves or rolls
with quick action yeast

'This is for those who can't always run to a shop to get fresh yeast. Since I've retired and started baking at home this quick-action yeast has been very useful.'

Yield: 7–8 bread rolls and 2 x ½ kg (1lb) loaves

500g (1lb 2oz) strong white bread flour

1 teaspoon dried milk powder

1 level teaspoon sea salt

1 level teaspoon sugar

2 x 7g sachets of quick-action yeast

2 eggs, beaten

1 tablespoon vegetable oil

300ml (10fl oz) tepid water

1 egg beaten with 1 teaspoon water for glazing

Toppings:
sesame or poppy seeds, grated parmesan or flaked almonds

- Preheat the oven to 425°F/220°C/Gas 7.
  Grease 2 x ½ kg (1lb) loaf tins, baking trays for rolls. Electric mixer with dough hook OR knead by hand. For full description of hand-kneading method see p.29.

- KNEADING DOUGH IN ELECTRIC MIXER: Put flour, milk powder, salt, sugar and yeast into the bowl. Using dough hook, start mixer on slow speed and add the eggs and oil, then most of the water. Check consistency and add more water if necessary. Knead for 5 minutes on a fast speed (knead 10 minutes by hand, see p.29). When it forms a smooth, pliable dough, remove and put into a greased bowl. Cover with a damp tea towel or clingfilm lightly greased with oil.

- PROVING: Leave in a warm (24-30°C/75-85°F), preferably humid place, out of draughts, but not near any naked heat, till doubled in size.

- SHAPING: Knock down and knead till smooth. Shape into rolls, plaits or loaves. Put on baking tray or into tins. Cover loosely with lightly oiled clingfilm and put back in the same warm, humid place to rise again.

- FINISHING: Brush with beaten egg and top with sesame or grated parmesan or flaked almonds.

- BAKING: Bake for 10–15 minutes until risen and browned for rolls – 30–40 minutes for ½ kg (1lb) tin loaves. Test for readiness: the base should sound hollow when tapped. Cool on rack. When completely cold wrap in clingfilm if storing.

Quick wholemeal loaves or rolls
with quick action yeast

'Using wholemeal flour, the dough will take a little longer to ferment and also may need a little more water to mix.'

Yield: 7–8 rolls, 2 x ½kg (1lb) loaves

500g (1lb 2oz) wholemeal bread flour

2 teaspoons sea salt

25g (1oz) milk powder

25g (1oz) sugar

2 x 7g sachets quick-action dried yeast

1 tablespoon treacle

1 tablespoon oil

1 egg, beaten

300ml (10fl oz) tepid water

1 egg beaten with 1 teaspoon water for glazing

Toppings:

toasted course oatmeal, rolled oats, dusting of granary flour, sesame or poppy seeds

- Preheat the oven to 425°F/220°C/Gas 7. Grease 2 x ½kg (1lb) loaf tins, baking trays for rolls. Electric mixer with dough hook OR knead by hand. For full description of hand-kneading method see p.29.

- KNEADING DOUGH IN ELECTRIC MIXER: Put flour, milk powder, salt, sugar and yeast into the bowl. Using the dough hook, start mixer on slow speed and add the eggs and oil. Then add most of the water. Check consistency and add more water if necessary. Knead for 5 minutes on a fast speed (knead 10 minutes by hand, see p.29). When it forms a smooth, pliable dough, remove and put into a greased bowl. Cover with a damp tea towel or clingfilm lightly greased with oil.

- PROVING: Leave in a warm (24-30°C/75-85°F), preferably humid place, out of draughts, but not near any naked heat, till doubled in size.

- SHAPING Knock down and knead till smooth. Shape into rolls, plaits or loaves. Put on baking tray or into tins. Cover loosely with lightly oiled clingfilm and put back in the same warm, humid place to rise again.

- FINISHING: Glaze with beaten egg and top with toasted coarse oatmeal, rolled oats, dusting of granary flour sesame or poppy seeds.

- BAKING: Bake for 10–15 minutes until risen and browned for rolls – 30–40 minutes for ½kg (1lb) tin loaves. Test for readiness: the base should sound hollow when tapped. Cool on rack. When completely cold wrap in clingfilm if storing.

Organic bread

'This is a slow-fermented bread which depends entirely for its mature flavour on the long fermentation and the good flavour of the stoneground flours.'

1kg (2lb 4oz) organic stoneground strong bread flour (white or wholemeal or any mix of the two)

2 teaspoons sea salt

125ml (4fl oz) organic extra virgin olive oil

750ml (27fl oz)
bottled water

15g (½ oz) fresh yeast creamed with a little tepid water or 1 packet quick-action yeast

1 egg beaten with 1 teaspoon water for glazing

Toppings:

sesame, pumpkin or sunflower seeds or oatflakes

- Preheat the oven to 425°F/220°C/Gas 7.
  Grease 3 x ½kg (1lb) loaf tins with olive oil and dust with sesame, pumpkin or sunflower seeds or oat flakes.
  Electric mixer with dough hook OR knead by hand. For full description of hand-kneading method see p.29.

- KNEADING AND FERMENTING DOUGH: Put the flour, salt, olive oil and two cups of water into the mixer bowl. Turn on at a slow speed and then add the yeast. Stop to check consistency and add more water to make a fairly soft sticky dough. Knead for 10 minutes with the dough hook in the mixer (knead 10 minutes by hand, see p.29). Put into a lightly greased bowl. Put into a lightly greased polythene bag. Secure end to keep out air and leave at room temperature overnight or longer (up to two days).

- SHAPING AND PROVING: Press air out of the dough and knead for a few minutes until it comes smooth and silky. Divide into three equal sized pieces – they should be about a ½kg (1lb) each. Then take each piece of dough and divide again into three. Roll each piece into a smooth ball, stretching the surface of the dough by tucking in round the base with your fingers as you work round the ball. Place three balls in each tin. Cover with lightly greased clingfilm and put in a warm place till doubled in size.

- BAKING: Brush with egg or milk and sprinkle more seeds or oat flakes on top. Bake for 35–40 minutes. Test for readiness: the base should sound hollow when tapped. Cool on rack. When completely cold wrap in clingfilm if storing.

Irish soda bread

'This is a smashing bread. I got this recipe from an Irish sous chef I met at the Triangle. I've also tried various versions in Ireland where they use a dark wholemeal which is almost like a malted meal with a very distinctive taste. In Dublin it was made with white flour and had dried fruit in it. At One Devonshire we always had it in the breakfast basket and also served it at dinner with pate. It's also very good fried with crisp bacon.'

Yield: One round, 4–8 triangles

175g (6oz) wholemeal flour

75g (3oz) strong white flour

25g (1oz) medium oatmeal

½ teaspoon bicarbonate of soda

½ teaspoon sea salt

**300-350ml (10-12fl oz) buttermilk
(or milk soured with the juice of a lemon)**

- Preheat the oven to 450°F/230°C/Gas 8. Grease and flour baking tray.

- MIXING: Put all the dry ingredients into a bowl and add most of the milk. Mix to a fairly soft consistency adding more milk if necessary.

- SHAPING: Place on a floured work surface. Dust with flour and roll out into a round about 2.5cm (1 inch) thick. Make two deep cuts dividing into four triangles. Dust with more flour.

- BAKING: Bake for about 20–30 minutes till risen and browned. Test for readiness: tap on the base when it should sound hollow. Cool on rack. Use immediately. Serve warm.

Scottish Girdle Baking

When English-based supermarket chains first opened in Scotland in the 1980s they discovered that unlike south of the border, a 'hotplate' was an essential item in their 'home' bakery section.

The lively market for scones, pancakes and crumpets – warm off the hotplate – dates back to the days when the most common method of baking for Scots was to hang a large round, square or oblong (depending on the size of their fire) metal plate (girdle) over the slow-burning peat fire for baking.

While the commercial baker has become an important source of girdle baking, home baking on the girdle (or other equivalent flat plate such as a large frying pan) is not a difficult operation. It also has a bake-to-order attraction which produces fresh, warm baking quickly, without heating an oven.

Girdle baking allows more control, since you can watch the baking as it cooks, learning to judge when it should be turned and when it is ready.

At some summer agricultural shows in Scotland, women from the WRI can be found in a tent with a queue out the door doing a roaring trade in hot-off-the-girdle pancakes and soda scones. They call it a 'continuous-baking' with expert girdle-bakers taking their turn of shifts throughout the day.

TO USE THE GIRDLE

Heat up slowly and evenly. Depending on the size of your girdle you may have to use two burners/hot plates and keep turning the girdle.

Test its heat by holding your hand about an inch from the surface when it should feel fairly hot, but not unbearably hot. Another test is to throw a little plain flour on the surface. This should turn light brown after a few minutes. If it turns brown immediately the girdle is too hot.

Grease the girdle lightly with oil. It may also be dusted with flour if you want a floury finish on scones. For pancakes and crumpets, re-grease the surface between each batch.

Soda Scones

'This is an unsweetened scone. The daily bread in some areas of Scotland where bread ovens were unknown.'

Yield: 2 rounds, 8 scones

225g (8oz) plain flour

1 level teaspoon bicarbonate of soda

1 level teaspoon cream of tartar

1 tablespoon vegetable oil

150ml (5fl oz) buttermilk or sweet milk soured with the juice of a lemon

Pinch of salt

- Pre-heat the girdle and grease lightly. Test heat with some flour which should turn a light brown in a few minutes. Also judge heat by holding your hand over the girdle when it should feel hot but not fiercely so.

- MIXING AND SHAPING: Sift the flour, bicarbonate of soda and cream of tartar into a bowl. Make a well in the centre and add the oil and sour milk and salt. Mix to a soft pliable dough. Do not overmix or the scones will shrink when baked. Turn out onto a floured board. Flour on top and divide into two. Roll each piece into a circle about 1cm thick.

- BAKING: Bake on the girdle for about 4–5 minutes on one side. Turn and bake on other side till cooked through. Fold in tea towel when cooked and serve warm with butter and strawberry jam.

Currant or Sultana Scones

'Funnily enough at One Devonshire the English and American guests went for these scones, whereas the Scots seemed to prefer a plain one.'

Yield: 24 with 5cm (2½ inch) cutter

225g (8oz) self-raising flour

25g (1oz) caster sugar

2 tablespoons vegetable oil

1 egg

150ml (5fl oz) milk

50g (2oz) currants

- Preheat the girdle and grease lightly. Test heat with some flour which should turn a light brown in a few minutes. Also judge heat by holding your hand over the girdle when it should feel hot but not fiercely so.

- MIXING AND SHAPING: Sift the flour into a bowl and add the sugar. Make a well in the centre. Mix the oil and egg together. Add, along with most of the milk and the currants. Mix to a soft dropping consistency, adding more milk if necessary. Leave to rest for 3 minutes. Roll out on a floured board to 1.5cm thick. Cut with a scone cutter into rounds.

- BAKING: Put onto the girdle and bake on one side for about five minutes until lightly browned. Turn and bake on the other side. Wrap in tea towel and place on a wrack. Serve warm.

Variation: Treacle Scones
- Add 3 tablespoons of treacle instead of the sugar. Mix with milk to dissolve.

Girdle Pancakes (*Dropped Scones*) and Girdle Crumpets

'Practice and patience are the secrets here. Don't be afraid to lose a few. It will all come right in the end.'

Yield: 18-20 Small pancakes – 10-15 crumpets

225g (8oz) self-raising flour

2 eggs, beaten

1 level tablespoon golden syrup

1 tablespoon vegetable oil

175ml (6fl oz) milk for pancakes

For crumpets:

Add 1 egg

250ml (9fl oz) milk

½ teaspoon bicarbonate of soda

- Heat girdle and grease. Test heat with some flour which should turn a light brown in a few minutes. Also judge heat by holding your hand over the girdle when it should feel hot but not fiercely so.

- TO MAKE PANCAKE MIX: Sift the flour into a bowl and make a well in the centre. Mix the eggs, syrup, oil and most of the milk. Add to the flour and mix to a thick 'pouring cream' consistency adding more milk if necessary.

- TO MAKE CRUMPET MIX: As for pancakes BUT add 1 extra egg and bicarbonate of soda which makes more bubbles while cooking. Use more milk – 375ml (12fl oz) – to make a runnier mixture. Sift flour and bicarbonate of soda into a bowl and make a well in the centre. Add the eggs, sugar and most of the milk. Mix to a thin cream consistency adding more milk if necessary.

- TO BAKE PANCAKES AND CRUMPETS: Drop in spoonfuls onto a hot girdle. Use a ladle for the crumpets which should spread to about 15mm (6 inches). When bubbles appear on the surface, turn. Crumpets should be thinner than pancakes with a lacy effect on one side. Pancakes are usually smaller. When bubbles appear on the top surface, turn. They should be an amber colour on both sides. Cool on a rack in a tea towel to keep warm and soft. Eat warm on the day they are baked. Serve pancakes with butter and jams. Fill crumpets with butter, lemon juice and sugar or jam or honey or syrup. Roll when cold like a brandy snap. If they crack the mixture has been too stiff.

Potato Scones

'You need a good starchy potato here. One that will soften well without going into lumps.'

Yield: 8

225g (8oz) floury potatoes, mashed

75g (3oz) plain flour

25g (1oz) butter

Pinch of salt

- Heat girdle and grease. Test heat with some flour which should turn a light brown in a few minutes. Also judge heat by holding your hand over the girdle when it should feel hot but not fiercely so.

- MIXING AND SHAPING: Put the mashed potato into a bowl and sift in the flour. Add the butter and salt. Mix to a smooth dough. It should be soft and pliable. Add some water if required. Divide into two, knead into round balls and roll into 2 circles 3-5mm thick. Cut each circle into four.

- BAKING: Bake on the girdle until brown on one side (about 3 minutes). Turn and brown the other side. Wrap in tea towel and serve warm with butter. Fry with bacon and eggs for a 'full' Scottish breakfast.

Speciality Breads

These are rich, sweet breads which can be made without changing the basic techniques of bread making. These range from a plain Italian Ciabatta to a very rich French Brioche and all follow the basic techniques of bread-making. The only difference is that, because some are very rich, including ingredients like spices, sugar and butter which inhibit the yeast rising, these are added after the basic dough is risen – as in the Chelsea, Selkirk Bannock and Danish Pastries.

Hot Cross Buns or Spiced Buns

'To make sure that the spice doesn't stop the yeast rising a foolproof method, known as 'sponge-and-dough' is used. It takes a bit longer, but it's worth it.'

For the 'starter':

350ml (12fl oz) tepid water

25g (1oz) fresh yeast

1 tablespoon sugar

25g (1oz) dried milk powder

75g (3oz) strong white flour

For the spice mix:

3 nutmegs

3 teaspoons whole allspice

1 stick cinnamon

1 teaspoon whole cloves

5cm/2inch piece of dried root ginger

For the buns:

650g (1lb 7oz) strong white flour

75g (3oz) vegetable fat

1 egg

50g (2oz) sugar

225g (8oz) dried mixed fruit

25g (1oz) spice mix

For the crosses:

100g (4oz) plain flour

3 tablespoons oil

Pinch of sugar

Water to mix

Egg for glazing

Finishing:

3–4 tablespoons apricot glaze or bun glaze

- Preheat the oven to 200°C/400°F/Gas 6. Grease and flour baking tins or use silicone paper.
  Electric mixer with dough hook OR knead by hand. For full description of hand-kneading method see p.29.

- TO MAKE THE STARTER: Mix everything together and leave in a warm place until the top is frothing and bubbling.

- TO MAKE THE SPICE MIX: Blend all the spices together in a coffee grinder and grind until fine. Store in an airtight jar. Label with the date and keep in a cool place and use within a month.

- TO MAKE THE BUNS: Put the flour into a mixing bowl and add the fat. Rub in and add the egg with sugar, dried fruit, starter mix and spice mix. Start the mixer on a slow speed and add more tepid water if necessary to make a softish dough or knead by hand. Beat on high speed for five minutes. Remove. Put into an oiled bowl, cover and put in a warm place to prove until it doubles in size. Knock back and shape into round buns. Put on an oiled tray. Cover and leave to rise until doubled again. Meanwhile make the mixture for the crosses: Put the flour, sugar and oil in a mixing bowl and add enough cold water to make an icing consistency. Put into piping bag.

- BAKING and FINISHING: Brush the buns with egg wash. Pipe on crosses. Bake till brown. Glaze with apricot glaze or bun glaze (see p.126) to give a finished shine.

Scottish Cookies

'Not to be confused with the American cookie, which is a biscuit. Or with a Devon split which it may be called in Scottish branches of English-based supermarkets. They are a favourite with a plain Scots high tea.'

Yield: 22–24

750g (1lb 10oz) strong bread flour

1 teaspoon salt

25g (1oz) sugar

125g (4oz) unsalted butter

2x7g packets quick-action yeast

125ml (4fl oz) milk

2 large eggs, beaten

200ml (7fl oz) tepid water

1 egg beaten with 1 teaspoon water for glazing

4 tablespoons apricot glaze

Variations:

Sugar Cookies

- Brush with apricot glaze. Dip in caster sugar.

Cream Cookies

- Split in two and fill with a teaspoon of jam and whipped cream. Dust with icing sugar.

Iced Cookies

- Make water icing: white, pink or chocolate and spread over top of cookies.

- Preheat the oven to 425°F/220°C/Gas 7. Grease and flour tins or use silicone paper.
  Electric mixer with dough hook OR knead by hand. For full description of hand-kneading method see p.29.

- KNEADING DOUGH IN MIXER: Put the flour, salt and sugar into the mixing bowl. Add the butter and rub through the mixture till it resembles fine breadcrumbs. (This can also be done in a blender.) Add the yeast and mix through. Mix the milk and eggs together. Make a well in the middle and add the milk mixture. Beat on slow speed till it comes together or knead by hand. Add enough water to make a softish dough. Then beat for four minutes till it becomes a smooth, silky pliable dough.

- SHAPING, PROVING AND BAKING: Divide into 22–24, 1½(50g)–2oz buns. Roll into round bun shapes. Place on baking tray leaving space to rise. Brush with beaten egg. Cover loosely with lightly oiled clingfilm. Leave in a warm (24–30°C/75–85°F), preferably humid place, out of draughts, but not near any naked heat, till doubled in size. Glaze again with beaten egg. Bake for 15–20 minutes till risen and browned. Test for readiness: should sound hollow when tapped on the base. Cool on rack.

- FINISHING PLAIN COOKIES: While still hot brush with apricot glaze (see p.126)

Chelsea Buns

'This square-shaped, sweet, fruity, sticky bun is a traditional London baking speciality, originally made by the Chelsea Bun House. Flavourings vary from plain – without spices and fruit – to more elaborate versions with mixed fruit. It is rolled up swiss-roll style, before it's cut into buns.'

Yield: 8-10

350g (12oz) strong bread flour

75g (3oz) caster sugar

75g (3oz) unsalted butter

2 x 7g quick-acting yeast

1 lemon, zest

125ml (4fl oz) tepid milk

2 large eggs, beaten

25g (1oz) currants

beaten egg for glazing

Final glazing:

2 tablespoons milk mixed with 2 tablespoons caster sugar

- Preheat the oven to 425°F/220°C/Gas 7. Grease and flour tins or use silicone paper.
  Electric mixer with dough hook OR knead by hand. For full description of hand-kneading method see p.29.

- KNEADING DOUGH IN MIXER: Put the flour, and half the sugar in the mixing bowl. Add half the butter and rub through the mixture till it resembles fine breadcrumbs (this can also be done in a blender). Add the yeast and lemon zest. Mix the milk and eggs. Make a well in the middle of the dough and add the milk mixture. Beat on slow speed till it comes together or knead by hand. Then beat for four minutes till it becomes a smooth, pliable dough.

- PROVING, SHAPING: Cover with lightly oiled clingfilm and put in a warm (24–30°C/75–85°F), preferably humid place, out of draughts, but not near any naked heat, till doubled in size for about 1 hour. Knock out air and knead till smooth. Roll out into a rectangle about 1cm (½ inch) thick. Spread with the remaining butter and sprinkle currants and half of the remaining sugar evenly over. Fold in three – a third up, a third down – turn a quarter then roll out again into the same rectangle shape. Sprinkle with the rest of the sugar. Wet one edge and roll up like a swiss roll. Cut into 8 slices about 2.5cm (1inch) thick. Place on their cut ends on baking trays in rows. Leave a little space between each bun, but not too much since the finished buns should have a square shape which occurs when their edges merge together during baking. Cover with lightly oiled clingfilm. Put in a warm place to rise.

- BAKING: When the buns have almost doubled in size and are touching, brush with egg wash and dust with caster sugar. Bake for 15–20 minutes till risen and browned. Glaze with milk and sugar when still warm. Cool on rack. Separate once they have cooled.

Selkirk Bannock

'This is a rich yeasted bannock, shaped like a round cob loaf and generously filled with sultanas, which is sold in bakers shops in the Scottish Borders. It has become so popular further afield that several Borders bakers have websites where they sell the bannock by mail order.'

1 packet fast-action yeast

450ml (16fl oz) tepid milk and water (50/50)

1kg (2 lb 4oz) strong plain flour

125g (4½ oz) butter

125g (4½ oz) vegetable fat

125g (4½ oz) sugar

500g (1lb 2oz) sultanas

1 teaspoon sea salt

1 egg beaten with 1 teaspoon water for glazing

- Pre-heat the oven to 425°F/220°C/Gas 7: bake for 15–20 minutes. Reduce to 375°F/190°C/Gas 5: bake for 20–30 minutes. Grease baking tray. Electric mixer with dough hook OR knead by hand. For full description of hand-kneading method see p.29.

- MAKING A 'SPONGE': Put the yeast into the mixer bowl with 100ml (4fl oz) of the tepid milk/water. Stir to dissolve and add 100g (4oz) flour. Cover with clingfilm and leave in a warm place (1–2 hours) till the yeast is frothing and bubbling.

- KNEADING THE DOUGH IN THE MIXER: Sift the remaining flour into the mixer bowl. Melt the butter and vegetable fat and add to the remaining milk. Add to flour along with sugar. Beat for five minutes (knead 10 minutes by hand). The dough should be smooth and silky. Cover with a damp cloth or clingfilm.

- PROVING: Put in a warm (24-30°C/75-85°F), preferably humid place, out of draughts, but not near any naked heat, till doubled in size – about 1 hour.

- ADDING FRUIT: Turn out the dough onto a floured surface and knead in the fruit. Shape into four small or two large buns. Place on a greased baking tray, cover with some lightly oiled clingfilm, and leave in the warm place again till they have doubled in size. Brush with egg glaze and put in a hot oven for 15–20 minutes then reduce the heat and bake for another 20–30 minutes. Test by sounding one with your knuckles on the base; it should sound hollow. (Large ones will take longer.)

French Brioche

'In France, bakers might put a little more butter in their brioche recipe. If you look at brioche in their windows, it's a dark colour on the outside and very crispy and flaky. Which is because of the amount of butter they use. Of course this makes it more difficult to work. The secret is to work very quickly. If you are too slow it will stick to your hands.'

Yield: 10 small brioche or one large

225g (8oz) strong bread flour

1 teaspoon sea salt

2 teaspoon sugar

1 packet easy-bake yeast

3 large eggs

2-3 tablespoons tepid water

100g (3½ oz) unsalted butter, softened

1 egg yolk beaten with 1 tablespoon milk for glazing

- Preheat the oven to 425°F/220°C/Gas 7. 10 small round, fluted brioche tins or 1 large round, fluted brioche tin, greased and floured.
  Electric mixer with dough hook OR knead by hand. For full description of hand-kneading method see p.29.

- KNEADING DOUGH IN MIXER: Put the flour, salt, sugar and yeast into the mixing bowl. On a slow speed, add the eggs one at a time till the dough begins to form or knead by hand. Test consistency. It should be softish but not too soft. Add water if necessary. Mix for about 10 minutes to develop the gluten when the dough will become smooth and elastic. Add the butter in small pieces. Keep scraping down the sides. The dough should now be smooth, glossy, soft and pliable.

- PROVING: Put the dough into an oiled bowl. Cover with lightly greased clingfilm and put in a warm (24–30°C/75–85°F), preferably humid place, out of draughts, but not near any naked heat, till doubled in size – about 2 hours. Knock out air and knead till smooth again. Cover and put in fridge for 2 hours. This makes it easier to shape.

- MOULDING AND SHAPING. For small buns: Cut dough into 10 pieces. Reserve a small piece for balls on top. Roll large pieces into balls and put into brioche tins. Roll small balls the size of your pinkie nail. Put the handle of a wooden spoon into cold water and make a hole in the top of the brioche. Place the small ball in the hole. Cover with lightly oiled clingfilm. Leave to prove in the same warm place. When they have risen to double their original size, brush with egg.

- For large bun: Remove a quarter of the dough and roll the remainder into a smooth round ball. Place in the base of the tin. Flour the work surface and shape the remaining quarter into the 'head'. It should be a rounded ball at one end and shaped like a long plug at the other. Make a hole in the middle of dough in the tin with your fingers and place the head into it with the rounded ball end on top. Cover with lightly greased clingfilm and leave to rise in a warm place. Brush with egg wash and make snips with scissors round the edge of large bun.

- BAKING: Bake for 10–12 minutes for small buns – 30 minutes for large bun – till risen and golden brown. They should sound hollow when tapped on the base. Unmould and cool on a rack.

Italian Ciabatta

'This popular rustic Italian bread depends for its popularity on a floury, crisp, golden crust and a moist, billowy crumb. Unlike other sour-dough breads it has a sweet, yeasty, champagne-like flavour, and is the ideal bread for mopping up Italian sauce-based dishes.'

Yield: 4 loaves

For the 'starter' (biga):

250ml (9fl oz) warm water

1 teaspoon fast-action yeast

350g (12oz) strong bread flour

For the dough:

1 teaspoon fast-action yeast

125ml (4fl oz) warm milk

250ml (9fl oz) warm water

1 tablespoon olive oil

1 teaspoon sea salt

500g (1lb 2oz) unbleached strong bread flour

- Preheat the oven to 425°F/220°C/Gas 7. Grease baking trays.
  Electric mixer with dough hook OR knead by hand. For full description of hand-kneading method see p.29.

- MAKING THE STARTER (BIGA): Put the water into a bowl and sprinkle over the yeast. Leave for about five minutes then start stirring in the flour, a handful at a time. Mixing with a wooden spoon to make a sticky dough. Cover with lightly greased clingfilm and leave to rise 15–24 hours at room temperature.

- KNEADING THE CIABATTA DOUGH: Put the milk into the mixer bowl and sprinkle over the yeast. Leave to stand for 10 minutes until creamy. Add the warm water, olive oil, salt and the starter. Mix on slow until blended or knead by hand. Then add the remaining flour. Knead with the dough hook until the dough becomes velvety, supple, very springy and moist. Add more warm water if necessary. Put into an oiled bowl and cover with lightly oiled clingfilm. Leave to rise for about an hour.

- SHAPING AND BAKING: Press air out of the dough and knead again until smooth. Cut the dough into 4 equal pieces on a well-floured board. Roll up each piece into a cylinder shape and then stretch out into a rectangle about 23 x 8cm (10 x 4 inch). Flour four pieces of baking silicone and place each loaf on top. Dimple the loaves with your fingers outstretched so that they look pockmarked. Cover with lightly oiled clingfilm. Leave to rise in a warm place until they are puffy but not doubled in size (they will rise more in the oven). Sprinkle baking silicone with cornmeal (polenta). Carefully invert each loaf onto the cornmeal. For a crisp crust, spray the inside of the oven with an atomiser. Bake for 20–30 minutes.

Danish pastries

'Though these are claimed by Denmark as their own speciality bread, they were originally made when the bakers of Copenhagen went on strike, about a century ago. Viennese bakers were imported and brought with them this original method of folding cold butter into yeast dough.'

Yield: 12 pastries

225g (8oz) strong bread flour

1/2 teaspoon salt

1 teaspoon sugar

25g (1oz) lard

2 x 7g sachets easy-bake yeast

1 large egg

125ml (4fl oz) milk

150g (5½ oz) butter

Filling:

Fresh, canned or bottled fruit including: peaches or nectarines, plums, apricots, apples, pears, figs

Ready to eat dried fruit such as: raisins, figs, cherries, apricots, candied peel

Pastry cream (crème patisserie) (see p.122)

1 egg beaten with 1 teaspoon water for glazing

Finishing:

apricot glaze, chopped walnuts, almonds, icing sugar or water icing

• Preheat the oven to 425°F/220°C/Gas 7. Grease baking trays.
Electric mixer with dough hook OR knead by hand. For full description of hand-kneading method see p.29.

KNEADING DOUGH IN MIXER: Put the flour, salt and sugar into the mixing bowl. Add the lard and rub through the mixture till it resembles fine breadcrumbs. Add the yeast. Mix the milk and eggs. Make well in the middle and add the milk mixture. Beat on slow speed till it comes together. Then beat for about four minutes till it becomes a smooth, pliable dough. Put into an oiled polythene bag and place in fridge for about 10 minutes. Meanwhile, with a palette knife soften the butter and shape it into a rectangle about 1cm (½ inch) thick.

• ROLLING: On a floured work surface roll out the dough to approximately 25cm (10 inch) square. Spread butter down the centre of the square to about 2.5cm (1 inch) from the edges. Fold the sides over the butter to overlap in the middle by about 1cm (½ inch). Seal the bottom and top with the rolling pin and roll out the dough to a rectangle about 45 x 15cm (18 x 16 inch). Fold up a third and down a third. Put in polythene bag and place in the fridge for 10 minutes to rest. Return to floured work surface and roll out. Repeat the folding, rolling and resting process twice more, ensuring that the dough is always rolled in a different direction each time. Leave in oiled poly bag for at least 4 hours or overnight before use.

- SHAPING: Divide the dough into two and roll each piece out to a large square about 5mm (¼ inch) thick. Cut each piece into six small squares. Brush off the excess flour.

- FILLING: Fill pastries with a few spoonfuls of pastry cream and top with fruit according to season/preference. Alternatively, fill with a few spoonfuls of marzipan.

- To make an ENVELOPE: Place filling in the middle. Take the four corners and fold in to the centre to make an envelope.

- To make a PINWHEEL: Cut a line from each corner into the middle to about 1 cm (½ inch). There are now four triangles joined at the centre. Place filling in the middle. Start at the bottom right hand corner of the square and lift the point of the bottom triangle over into the centre. Continue round the square, lifting the bottom right hand corner of each triangle into the centre. Repeat with other pastries.

- To make TWISTS: Roll out pastry and spread with jam or lemon curd. Fold the bottom third up and the top third down to make three layers. Slice into strips about 2.5cm (1 inch) wide. Give each strip a half twist as it is placed on the baking tray.

- PROVING: Cover loosely with lightly oiled clingfilm and put in a warm (24–30°C/75–85°F), preferably humid, place which is out of draughts but not near any naked heat, till doubled in size. Brush exposed pastry lightly with egg.

- BAKING: Bake for 25–30 minutes till golden brown.

- FINISHING: Brush with apricot glaze and sprinkle with chopped walnuts or almonds. Or, dust with icing sugar. Or, dribble over some water icing. Serve warm.

Muffins, Scones, Buns and Teabreads

Along with pancakes, maple syrup and crispy bacon, Americans eat these hot-out-the-oven muffins as regular breakfast items. The high-domed American muffin bears no resemblance, however, to an English muffin which is a flat, yeasted, girdle-baked teabread.

Such is the popular appeal of the American variety, that Hot Muffin cafés in the UK now operate a continuous-baking system of hot, freshly baked muffins for eating-in or taking away. And not just for breakfast, but also for elevenses, lunch, teabreaks, dinner and supper.

These are the muffins for the quick-and-easy baker. Like quickly-made teabread, they depend entirely on chemicals to leaven the batter and nothing more than chucking all the ingredients into a bowl to mix.

Scones are a stiffer version which stand on their own without any help from a tin. Rock buns are even stiffer, while Paris, London and Jam buns are a little softer. Teabreads are the cake version of the muffin, quickly and easily made by adding all the ingredients together and, again, depending entirely on chemical raising agents.

While their advantage is their saving of time and labour, their disadvantage is a poor keeping quality. So bake and eat warm.

Fresh Berry Muffins

'The traditional berry in American muffins is the blueberry though other soft fruits such as raspberries, plums, mangos, peaches, necatrines and pears are also used. These are the muffins I made at 3am in the hotel for the breakfast basket. They keep and eat well and have a homemade taste, unlike the commercial mixes made in bakeries.'

Yield: 12

250g (9oz) self-raising flour

75g (3oz) caster sugar

75g (3oz) softened butter, unsalted

25g (1oz) vegetable fat

1 teaspoon vanilla extract

125ml (4fl oz) milk

2 eggs

225g (8oz) fresh fruit or sultanas

1 tablespoon granulated sugar

- Preheat the oven to 425°F/220°C/Gas 7. Grease and flour a 12-size muffin tin or use muffin paper cases.

- MIXING: Put the flour into the mixing bowl with the sugar and beat for 30 seconds to incorporate. Add the butter, fat, vanilla, milk and eggs and beat for a few minutes till creamy and light. It should be a soft dropping consistency. Stir in fresh fruit or sultanas. Drop in spoonfuls filling the paper cases or tins nearly to the top. Sprinkle the tops lightly with granulated or demerara sugar.

- BAKING: Bake for approximately 15–20 minutes. Leave in the tin for five minutes before turning out. Eat warm.

Variations

Apple & Date Muffins

- Use 225g (8oz) tart cooking apples, peeled, cored and chopped finely. Mix through the mixture. Put a whole stoned date in the bottom of each muffin tin. Sprinkle tops with demerara sugar before baking.

Poppy Seed Muffins

- Use 50g (2oz) poppy seeds and 25g (1oz) icing sugar. Boil in 150ml (5fl oz) water to reduce liquid almost completely. Pour into a dish and leave to cool overnight. Rub to loosen. Mix through the mixture and sprinkle some seeds on top.

Doughnuts *(non-yeast)*

'The mixture here must be a bit stiffer than scones since it's to be deep fried in oil and would break up if it was too soft.'

Yield: 6-8

2 tablespoons vegetable oil

50g (2oz) sugar

1 egg

125ml (4fl oz) milk

225g (8oz) self-raising flour, sifted

Caster sugar and mixed spice for dredging
Oil for deep frying

- Pre-heat the oil to 320-340°F

- MIXING AND SHAPING: Put the oil, sugar and egg into a mixing bowl with a little of the milk and mix well. Add the flour and mix. Add enough milk to make a soft, but firm dough. Do not over mix. Turn out onto a floured board and dust with flour. Roll out to 1cm (½ inch) thick. Cut into rounds with a cutter. Remove the centre with a 2cm (¾ inch) cutter. Leave to rest for ten minutes.

- DEEP FRYING: Test the oil with a small piece of dough when it should turn an amber colour. Put doughnuts into the hot fat, turning and browning on both sides. Place on cooking rack then dredge in caster sugar mixed with a little mixed spice.

Date and Walnut Banana Loaf

'The dates and walnuts can be omitted for a plainer cake.'

250g (8oz) plain flour

1 level teaspoon bicarbonate of soda

150g (5oz) soft brown sugar

75g (3oz) unsalted butter, softened

2 eggs, beaten

2 large bananas, mashed

2-3 tablespoons milk

100g (4oz) chopped walnuts

175g (6oz) stoned and quartered dates

- Preheat the oven to 350°F/180°C/Gas 4. Grease or line a 21 x 11cm (8 x 5inch) loaf tin.

- MIXING AND BAKING: Put the flour and bicarbonate of soda into a bowl with the sugar. Beat for about 30 seconds. Add butter, eggs, bananas and milk. Beat until smooth and creamy and a soft dropping consistency. Add a little hot water if it is too stiff. Add walnuts and mix in. Place the dates evenly over the base of the tin and pour the mixture on top. Bake for 45–50 minutes. Test for readiness with a skewer which should come out clean.

- TO STORE: wrap in clingfilm and keep in the fridge. Will keep up to 14 days becoming moister as it matures.

Oven Scones

The scone belongs to the British family of small tea cakes. In Scotland it is pronounced 'skawn' as in 'gone', while in England it becomes a 'scowne' as in 'own'.

They need not be limited to afternoon teatime.

Savoury scones make good accompaniments to soups. They are also good at the end of a meal with cheese. Also for an impromptu breakfast/brunch.

'There are three ways of rising this scone, the most traditional is with buttermilk and soda. This gives a most moist, spongy texture. The other methods make a drier scone.'

Yield: 8 quarters or 12–24 depending on thickness and cutter size

Either:
225g (8oz) plain flour

1 teaspoon bicarbonate of soda

1 teaspoon cream of tartar

125ml (4fl oz) buttermilk, or fresh milk soured with the juice of half a lemon

or
225 (8oz) plain flour

2 teaspoons baking powder

125ml (4fl oz) fresh milk

or
225g (8oz) self-raising cake flour

125ml (4fl oz) milk

50g (2oz) butter or 2 tablespoons oil

1 egg, beaten

- Preheat the oven to 450°F/230°C/Gas 8. Grease and flour baking tins or use silicone paper.

- MIXING AND SHAPING: Sift flour and raising agent into a bowl and rub in the butter or blend in blender. Make a well in the centre and add the milk and egg. Mix to an elastic consistency. Dust with flour and knead lightly on a floured working surface. Roll out to 2.5cm (1 inch) thick. Either into two rounds, cut into four quarters or cut with a cutter. Dust with flour and bake till risen and golden brown, 15–20 minutes. Wrap in towel, place on rack and serve slightly warm with butter and jam.

Cream Scones

'Rich, dense scones with a good flavour.'

125g (4oz) fine plain flour

125g (4oz) self-raising cake flour

½ teaspoon bicarbonate of soda

2 tablespoons oil

200ml (7fl oz) soured cream

1 egg, beaten

- Follow method for sweet milk scones.

Sultana Scones

- Follow method for sweet milk or cream scones. Use a wholemeal self-raising flour. Add 1 tablespoon soft brown sugar and 75g (3oz) sultanas.

Treacle Scones

- Follow method for sweet milk or cream scones. Add 2 tablespoons black treacle or molasses with the milk

Honey Scones

- Follow method for sweet milk or cream scones. Add 2 tablespoons flavoured honey with the milk.

Cheese Scones

- Follow method for sweet milk or cream scones. Add 150g (5oz) mature Scottish cheddar, finely grated, with a large pinch of cayenne pepper.

Strawberry Shortcake

'American invention of warm scone, whipped cream and ripe strawberries.'

Follow method for sweet milk or cream scones

750g (1lb 10oz) ripe strawberries
3 tablespoons caster sugar
Juice of 1 lemon
25g (1oz) softened unsalted butter
300ml (10fl oz) whipping cream, whipped

- PREPARING THE BERRIES: Wash and hull the berries. Slice roughly and cover with sugar and lemon juice. Leave for at least an hour, turning once or twice.

- SHAPING THE SCONE AND BAKING: Roll the scone dough out to a large round about 25cm (10 inches). Bake for 13–20 minutes.

- FINISHING: Place scone on rack for 5 minutes. When almost cold, split and butter one half. Place onto serving dish. Pile about three-quarters of the cream on top and then three-quarters of the berries. Place other half of scone on top. Cover with remaining cream and berries and serve for afternoon tea or as a dessert.

Scone Pizza

'I've eaten pizzas in Paris and Amsterdam – all different. The original Italian pizzas are baked in special ovens and have a very crunchy base. So far, I've never come across anyone making a scone-based pizza. Have a go. Variety is the spice of life.'

Yield: 4

225g (8oz) self-raising flour
Pinch of salt
½ teaspoon dried mustard powder
50g (2oz) butter
125ml (4fl oz) milk

Topping:
1 tablespoon tomato purée
500g (1lb 2oz) tomatoes, finely sliced
1 teaspoon oregano or basil
salt and pepper
225g (8oz) grated mozzarella cheese
8 anchovy fillets
12 black olives
1 tablespoon oil

- Preheat the oven to 425°F/220°C/Gas 7. Grease and flour baking tins or use silicone paper.

- MIXING AND SHAPING: Sift the flour into a bowl and add the salt and mustard. Rub in the butter. Make a well in the centre and add the milk. Mix to a fairly soft dough. Turn out onto a floured board and roll into a round 25cm (10 inch). Bake for 10 minutes.

- FINISHING/BAKING: Spread dough with tomato paste. Cover with tomatoes. Sprinkle with oregano or basil. Season with salt and pepper. Cover with grated cheese and decorate on top with anchovies and olives. Brush with oil. Bake till melted and lightly browned on top for 10–12 minutes.

Paris Buns

Yield: 8–10

225g (8oz) self-raising flour
75g (3 oz) butter
75g (3oz) caster sugar
1 egg
50g (2oz) sultanas
100ml (3fl oz) milk
1 egg mixed with 1 teaspoon water for glazing
1 tablespoon sugar nibs

- Preheat the oven to 470°F/230°C/Gas 8. Grease trays lightly with oil or use silicone paper.

- MIXING AND BAKING: Sieve the flour into a bowl. Rub in the butter (or mix in blender) till the mixture resembles fine breadcrumbs. Add the sugar, eggs, sultanas and most of the milk. Mix to a fairly stiff dough (a fork should stand up in the mixture). Add more milk if necessary. Drop buns onto the tray in spoonfuls, spacing well. Glaze with beaten egg and sprinkle with sugar nibs. Bake till risen and browned 15–20 minutes.

Jam Buns

Yield: 8–10

225g (8oz) self-raising flour
75g (3 oz) butter
75g (3oz) caster sugar
1 egg
90ml (3fl oz) milk
1 egg mixed with 1 teaspoon water for glazing
2 tablespoons jam
1 tablespoon granulated sugar

- Preheat the oven to 470°F/230°C/Gas 8. Grease trays lightly with oil or use silicone paper.

- MIXING AND BAKING: Sieve the flour into a bowl. Rub in the butter (or mix in blender) till the mixture resembles fine breadcrumbs. Add the sugar, egg, and most of the milk. Mix to a fairly stiff dough. Add more milk if necessary. Roll mixture into round balls. Place on baking tray. Make an indent in the top and fill with a small spoonful of jam. Brush round the sides of the bun with egg and sprinkle with granulated sugar. Bake till risen and browned, 15–20 minutes.

Rock Buns

Yield: 8–10

225g (8oz) self-raising flour
75g (3 oz) butter
50g (2oz) caster sugar
1 egg
75g (3oz) currants
50ml (2fl oz) milk
1 egg beaten with 1 teaspoon water for glazing
1 tablespoon granulated sugar

- Preheat the oven to 470°F/230°C/Gas 8.
  Grease trays lightly with oil or use silicone paper.

- MIXING AND BAKING: Sieve the flour into a bowl. Rub in the butter (or mix in blender) till the mixture resembles fine breadcrumbs. Add the sugar, egg, currants and most of the milk. Mix to a fairly stiff dough. Add more milk if necessary. Drop buns onto the tray in spoonfuls, spacing well. Glaze with beaten egg and sprinkle with granulated sugar. Rough up the sides with two forks. Bake till risen and browned, 15–20.

London Buns

Yield: 8–10

225g (8oz) self-raising flour
75g (3 oz) butter
50g (2oz) caster sugar
1 egg
50g (2oz) chopped mixed peel
1 lemon, zest
100ml (3fl oz) milk
Lemon or orange peel for top
1 egg beaten with 1 teaspoon water for glazing
1 tablespoon granulated sugar

- Preheat the oven to 470°F/230°C/Gas 8.
  Grease trays lightly with oil or use silicone paper.

- MIXING AND BAKING: Sieve the flour into a bowl. Rub in the butter (or mix in blender) till the mixture resembles fine breadcrumbs. Add the sugar, eggs, mixed peel, lemon zest and most of the milk. Mix to a soft dough. Add more milk if necessary. Drop buns onto the tray in spoonfuls, spacing well. Place two pieces of orange or lemon peel on top. Glaze with beaten egg and sprinkle with sugar. Bake till risen and browned, 15–20 minutes.

Gingerbread

'This is a very rich, moist gingerbread which is none the worse if it sinks a little in the middle.'

175g (6oz) unsalted butter, chopped small

175g (6oz) soft dark brown sugar

175g (6oz) black treacle

3 heaped teaspoons ground ginger

3 heaped teaspoons ground cinnamon

2 eggs, beaten

175g (6oz) regular plain flour (not for cakes), sifted

1 teaspoon bicarbonate of soda, sifted

200ml (7fl oz) buttermilk or fresh milk soured with the juice of a lemon OR natural yoghurt

Optional:

50g (1oz) crystallised ginger, finely diced and/or 50g (1oz) pistachio nuts

• Preheat the oven to 350°F/180°C/Gas 4. Grease and line a square 20cm (8 inch) tin.

• MIXING: Put butter, sugar, treacle and spices into a pan and heat gently to melt the butter and soften the treacle. When cool, beat in the eggs and add the ginger or pistachio nuts. Then stir in the flour sifted with soda. Mix together. Finally add the soured milk/yoghurt and mix in. It should make a fairly runny consistency.

• BAKING: Pour into the tin and bake for 45–60 minutes. Test with a skewer for readiness, it should come out clean.

Granny Loaf

'A boiled fruit cake which is quick and easy to make. Also a good keeping cake. This is one of Catherine's recipes which I used for afternoon tea at One Devonshire.'

300ml (10fl oz) hot water

150g (5oz) soft or dark brown sugar

75g (3oz) unsalted butter

350g (12oz) mixed dried fruit

2 teaspoons mixed spice

150g (5½ oz) plain flour, sifted

150g (5½ oz) self-raising flour, sifted

1 level teaspoon bicarbonate of soda, sifted

2 eggs

• Preheat the oven to 350°F/180°C/Gas 4. Grease or line a 21 x 11cm (8 x 5 inch) loaf tin.

• MIXING: Put water, sugar, butter, dried fruit and mixed spice into a pan. Simmer for 3 minutes then leave to cool. Add flours and bicarbonate of soda along with eggs and mix to a soft dropping consistency. Pour into baking tin.

• BAKING: Bake for about 1½ hours. Test for readiness with a skewer, which should come out clean.

Biscuits

The Scots are great biscuit lovers – consuming around 15% more per year than the rest of the UK. The National Library of Scotland in Edinburgh was largely built with 'biscuit' money from many famous Scottish biscuit companies. This biscuit legacy also includes good biscuit recipes and, of course, shortbread.

Classed by the Scottish Association of Master Bakers as an 'item of flour confectionery' and not a 'biscuit', every Scottish baker has a preferred shortbread recipe. These range in texture from hard-and-crunchy to soft and melting. While the texture can be manipulated according to your preference, the taste variation in shortbread is largely due to the quality and type of butter. Buy a good butter (see p.23) and you will have a good shortbread, though there is also skill in the blending and firing.

Shortbread Fingers

'This was the recipe I used at One Devonshire. It brought me great fame. I hope it does the same for you. Texturewise it's in the soft-and-melting category. Final success will always depend on slow, careful baking.

But remember, if you never burnt anything, you never made anything.'

Yield: 25–30 thin fingers, 15–20 thick or 3 x 15cm (6 inch) round shortbread moulds

225g (8oz) plain flour, sifted
110g (4oz) cornflour, sifted
110g (4oz) icing sugar, sifted
225g (8oz) unsalted butter, softened and cut into small pieces

Dredging:
caster sugar

- Preheat the oven to 325°F/150°C/Gas 3. Depth of shortbread for thick fingers 2cm (3/4 inch). For thin fingers 5mm (1/4 inch). Dust baking tin or shortbread mould lightly with flour.

- MIXING BY HAND: Sift the flour onto the work surface. Begin with the butter and sugar, kneading all the sugar into the butter. Then add a little flour and gradually work into the butter and sugar. Continue adding the flour until the mixture becomes firm and pliable but not too stiff. It should not be difficult to roll out and should not crack.

- MIXING BY MACHINE: Put all the ingredients into the mixing bowl. Put on a slow speed and mix until the dough begins to come together. Then raise speed a little until it forms a smooth dough. Test the consistency and add more flour if it is too soft.

- SHAPING THIN fingers: Roll out to 5mm (1/4 inch) and cut in fingers approx 6.5cm (2 1/2 inch) long, and 2.5cm (1 inch) wide. Put onto baking tin. Mark all over with a fork to prevent rising. Rest in a cool place for 1 hour before baking.

- SHAPING THICK fingers: Roll out into large square or press into tin. It should be approximately 2cm (3/4 inch) thick. Mark in lengths 7.5cm (3 inch) long. 2.5cm (1 inch) wide. Mark with a fork to prevent rising. Rest in a cool place for 1 hour before baking.

- SHAPING INTO LARGE ROUND: Roll out into large round about 2cm (3/4 inch) thick. Place on baking tray. Pinch edge with first finger and thumb to decorate or use the flat edge of a fork to mark the edge. Mark into triangles and mark all over with a fork to prevent rising. Rest in a cool place for 1 hour before baking.

- USING A SHORTBREAD MOULD: Divide dough equally into three and press one piece into the floured mould. Run a rolling pin over the top to level it. With fingertips, pull out edges all round so they are not ragged and come away cleanly. Reverse and – holding your hand underneath to catch the shortbread as it comes out – knock out dough by hitting the edge of the mould on the edge of a table. It may be necessary to hit it in several places before it comes out. Place on baking tin and mark with a fork. Repeat with other two pieces of dough. Rest for 1 hour in a cool place before baking.

- BAKING: Bake till evenly golden brown. Thin fingers will take 20–30 minutes, thicker fingers, round and mould, 45–50 minutes. Dredge with sugar. While still warm, cut thick fingers in half down the middle with a sharp knife. Cut each half into fingers. Remove from tin and put to cool on a rack. Store in airtight container.

Petticoat Tails

'These were first made by high class Edinburgh bakers and take their name from the shape of the petticoat hoops worn by women in the 19th century. It's thought that they were first made as a delicate shortbread, suitable for ladies' afternoon teas, while men preferred a thicker, crunchier version.'

Yield: 1 round

200g (7oz) plain flour

50g (2oz) icing sugar

75g (3oz) butter, softened

25g (1oz) vegetable fat

Dredging:
caster sugar

- Preheat the oven to 325°F/150°C/Gas 3. Dust baking tin lightly with flour.

- MIXING: Put all the ingredients into the mixing bowl. Put on a slow speed and mix until the dough begins to come together. Then raise speed a little until it forms a smooth dough. Roll out to a large round about 5mm (¼ inch) thick. Crimp the edges with your first finger and thumb. Mark all over with a fork. Then cut out a circle from the centre. Divide the rest of the circle into 12 to 18 wedge-shaped biscuits – 'petticoat tails'. Place on baking tray.

- BAKING: Bake for 20 minutes then raise the heat to 350°F/180°C/Gas 4 and continue baking till golden brown. Sprinkle with sugar while still warm. Remove from tin and put to cool on a rack. Store in an airtight container.

Parkins

'A popular Scottish teatime biscuit.'

Yield: 12–15 biscuits

100g (3½ oz) plain flour, sifted

125g (4½ oz) oatmeal

40g (1½ oz) soft brown sugar

50g (2oz) soft vegetable cooking fat

1 teaspoon each of ground ginger, ground cinnamon and mixed spice

1 level teaspoon bicarbonate of soda

2 tablespoons golden syrup

1 medium egg, beaten

Topping:
12–15 blanched almonds

- Preheat the oven to 350°F/180°C/Gas 4. Grease baking sheet lightly with oil.

- MIXING AND BAKING: Mix all the ingredients together to make a stiff but pliable dough. Add more egg if necessary. Divide into 12–15 pieces, roll into round balls then leave to rest for 5 minutes. Place a split almond on top of each piece. Put onto baking tray leaving room for spreading, then bake for ten minutes till golden brown on top. Cool and store in an airtight tin.

Abernethy Biscuits

'A "light" shortbread, made with less fat, they are named – not after the town of Abernethy – but after the distinguished Scots surgeon, Dr John Abernethy (1764-1831) who got his local baker to make them as a "health" biscuit to give to his patients.'

Yield: 8 biscuits

100g (3½ oz) plain flour
1 teaspoon baking powder
30g (1oz) soft vegetable cooking fat
30g (1oz) icing sugar
1 tablespoon milk
1 beaten egg

- Preheat the oven to 350°F/180°C/Gas 4. Grease baking tin lightly with oil.

- MIXING AND BAKING: Put the flour, baking powder, fat and sugar into a bowl. Rub in the fat. Add the milk and egg to make a soft but pliable dough. Divide into 8 pieces, roll into balls, then leave to rest for 3–4 minutes. Roll out to 5mm(¼ inch), then mark with a fork and place on baking tray. Bake for 20 minutes until golden brown. Cool on a rack and store in an airtight tin.

Oatcakes

'These are useful for serving with cheese, or for breakfast with honey or marmalade.'

Yield: 12

200g (7oz) medium oatmeal
50g (2oz) plain flour, sifted
40g (1½ oz) softened vegetable cooking fat or butter
75ml (2½ fl oz) boiling water
1 teasp honey or sugar

- Preheat the oven to 350°F/180°C/Gas 4. Lightly oil two baking sheets.

- MIXING AND BAKING: Put the oatmeal and flour into a bowl and make a well in the centre. Measure the boiling water and cut up the fat into small pieces. Add to the boiling water and heat through in a pan, (this can also be heated in the microwave) adding the honey. Pour into the dry ingredients. Mix until it forms a soft pliable dough. Add more boiling water if it is too stiff. It should not crack when rolled out. Divide dough into three pieces. While still hot, roll quickly into three rounds about 18cm (7 inches) diameter. Cut each round into 4 triangles (farls). Place on baking tin and bake for 40 minutes until they turn a light sandy colour. Cool on a wrack and store in an airtight tin.

Ginger Snaps

'A teatime biscuit.'

Yield: 25-30 biscuits

150g (5½ oz) plain flour

25g (1oz) self-raising flour

1 teaspoon bicarbonate of soda

2 teaspoons ground ginger

50g (2oz) softened vegetable fat

75g (3oz) soft brown sugar

1 tablespoon golden syrup

1 egg

- Preheat the oven to 350°F/180°C/Gas 4. Lightly oil two baking sheets.

- MIXING AND BAKING: Sieve flours, soda and ginger into a bowl. Add the fat, sugar and syrup. Beat till smooth. Add the egg, and mix till smooth. Let it rest for a couple of minutes. Roll into a long sausage shape and roll in demerara sugar. Leave in a cool place to harden. When firm, slice into 25–30 pieces. Place on greased baking tin and bake for 7–8 minutes. Cool and store in an airtight tin.

Chocolate and Ginger Cookies

'These are "dropped" American cookies with a soft centre which are quick and easy to make with no rolling or shaping.'

Yield: 40

175g (6oz) butter

175g (6oz) caster sugar

1 egg

90ml (3fl oz) milk, 6 tablespoons

75g (3oz) plain flour

75g (3oz) self-raising flour

50g (2oz) best quality plain chocolate grated

125g (4oz) crystallised ginger, chopped finely

50g (2oz) best quality dark chocolate chips

- Pre-heat the oven to 350°F/180°C/Gas 4. Grease baking tray with oil.

- MIXING AND BAKING: Beat the butter and sugar till soft and fluffy. Add the egg and milk, and mix in. Add flours, chocolate, ginger and chocolate chips. Mix to a soft consistency. Drop in spoonfuls on baking tray, leaving space for spreading. Bake for 12–15 minutes till browned.

Oat and Walnut Biscuits

'An easy-to-make biscuit. They have a lovely nutty chewiness and a good buttery flavour. The original recipe came from Australia where they are known as Anzac biscuits. They are made for Anzac Day which celebrates the Australia and New Zealand Army Corps (ANZAC) who fought in the invasion of the Gallipoli peninsula in 1915.'

125g (4oz) butter

2 tablespoons golden syrup

1 level teaspoon bicarbonate of soda

1½ tablespoon water

75g (3oz) plain flour

50g (2oz) coconut

125g (4oz) rolled oats

125g (4oz) caster sugar

50g (2oz) chopped walnuts

- Preheat the oven to 350°F/180°C/Gas 4. Lightly oil two baking sheets.

- MIXING: Put the butter in a pan and add the syrup, melt together. Leave to cool. Mix the bicarbonate of soda with the water, then add to the cooled butter mixture. Put the flour, coconut, rolled oats, sugar and walnuts into a bowl. Make a well in the centre and add the butter mixture. Mix well to a stiff paste. Roll into walnut sized balls.

- BAKING: Place on baking sheet leaving space for the biscuits to spread. Bake for 15–20 minutes. Cool on a rack.

Viennese Biscuits

'A sophisticated biscuit for special occasions.'

Yield: 13–14 biscuits

225g (8oz) unsalted butter, softened

75g (3oz) icing sugar

225g (8oz) plain flour

1 teaspoon vanilla extract

Filling:

Butter cream (see p.123)

175g (6oz) melted best quality plain chocolate for dipping

- Preheat the oven to 450°F/230°C/Gas 8. Line two baking trays with parchment or silicone.

- TO MAKE: Put all the ingredients into the mixing bowl and beat till thoroughly mixed to a smooth paste. Continue to beat for 2 minutes. Put into a piping bag with a 3cm (1¼ inch) star tube and pipe onto baking sheet in small rounds or long fingers.

- BAKING: Put into the oven and bake for about 10 minutes until golden brown.

- FINISHING: Sandwich biscuits with buttercream and dip one end into melted chocolate. Leave on rack till hardened.

- STORING: In an airtight tin.

Brandy Snaps

'The most decorative way to mould these is over the end of a wine glass. I used to paint the insides with plain melted chocolate so we could put fruit and ices into the basket.'

Yield: 17–20

65g (2½ oz) caster sugar

25g (1oz) softened unsalted butter

25g (1oz) golden syrup

25g (1oz) plain flour

1 level teaspoon ground ginger

1 teaspoon brandy

Melted best quality plain chocolate for brushing insides (optional)

- Preheat the oven to 400°F/200°C/Gas 6. Grease baking tray or line with parchment or silicone.

- MIXING AND BAKING: Beat the sugar and butter with the syrup, then add the flour, ginger and brandy. Beat till smooth. Drop in small spoonfuls on baking tray allowing enough space between each for spreading. Bake for 10 minutes till lightly browned. Turn off oven. Meanwhile oil rolling pin. When ready, mould biscuits over rolling pin till cool and set. Keep remaining biscuits warm in the oven till ready to mould.

- TO MAKE A BRANDY SNAP BASKET: Keeping biscuits warm in the oven, take one biscuit and place on top of upturned wine glass. Press the edges down to make the basket shape. Remove when set and continue with remaining biscuits. Brush inside with melted plain chocolate before filling with fruit, ices etc.

- STORING: Store in an airtight box.

Cakes

These are divided into three categories according to three different methods of mixing.

The first – flour batter – is a method widely used in commercial baking, and commercial cake mixes, where it's possible to mix everything together without creaming the butter and sugar. It works best if the flour used is a specially fine self-raising flour and/or is specially sifted.

The second – egg batter – is a method using air incorporated when beating eggs. Best results are also achieved when using specially fine plain flour for cakes and/or specially sifted.

The third – sugar batter – is the traditional method of creaming the butter and sugar. A more time-consuming method, but best used for larger cakes. Most successful results are also achieved when a specially fine plain flour and/or sifted for cakes is used.

FLOUR BATTER CAKES

This is the fastest method of making cakes. Its advantage is that all the ingredients are beaten together without the time-consuming stages of beating the eggs with sugar or creaming the sugar and butter. It also avoids the problem of the eggs curdling the sugar and butter mixture.

It may be the quickest and the easiest method, but is the finished quality compromised as a result?

This depends, largely, on the quality of the flour. 'Special' self-raising flours will give the best results. A 'regular' self-raising flour will also work well though the texture will be a little coarser.

Variously described as 'ideal for cakes and scones', or 'light', or 'supreme sponge', or 'extra fine', these special cake flours make a better textured cake using this method because they have such a high starch content and a low gluten content.

Until a few years ago this flour was only available to professional bakers in the UK though it has always been available for home bakers in America where it was originally always essential for their light-as-air 'angel cake' recipe (*see* Ingredients p.22).

DOS AND DON'TS

- Preferably use a special cake or sponge self-raising flour.
- Always use caster sugar.
- All the dry ingredients should be at room temperature and the eggs, butter and milk slightly warmed.
- Use an electric mixer or hand held beater on high speed
- Cool cake in the tin for 10 minutes to allow it to 'set'.

Vanilla Butter Sponge *(basic mix)*

- BASIC METHOD: Put the cake flour and caster sugar into a bowl and mix with an electric beater for 30 seconds. This brings the flour and sugar particles closer together when the sugar crystals puncture the flour particles allowing more liquid to be absorbed faster.

Add three-quarters of the eggs/liquid along with the butter, which has been softened, and beat for about 90 seconds until it becomes creamy and light. This is when the strength of the cake is developed. Add the remaining liquid and beat for another 30 seconds.

250g (9oz) self-raising cake flour

250g (9oz) caster sugar

250g (9oz) unsalted butter, softened

4 eggs, beaten

2–3 tablespoons milk

2 teaspoons vanilla extract

- Preheat the oven to 350°F/180°C/Gas 4. Line 23–25cm (9–10 inch) round cake tin; or 2 x 20cm (8 inch) sandwich tins with silicone baking paper, or foil, or grease and flour.

- HEATING THE EGGS: Put eggs, still in their shells, into a bowl of very hot, but not boiling water. Leave for 2 minutes to heat the eggs without cooking.

- MIXING: Sift flour into a bowl and add sugar. Beat with an electric beater for about 30 seconds. Add butter. Mix the eggs and 2 tablespoons milk together and add about three-quarters of this mixture to the flour, sugar and butter. Beat for about 90 seconds till the mixture becomes light and creamy. Scrape down the sides. Add the remaining eggs, milk and vanilla and beat for another 30 seconds. Add remaining tablespoon of milk if necessary. Pour into prepared tin(s).

- BAKING: Bake large cake for 60–70 minutes or until a skewer inserted into the centre comes out clean. Bake sandwich cakes for 25–30 minutes. Cool in the tin(s) for 10 minutes, then turn out onto a rack.

Chocolate Coated Butter Sponge

- Coat with Chocolate Cream Icing: Melt 200g (7oz) best quality plain chocolate. Put 200ml (7fl oz) double cream into a pan and heat through. Pour over the chocolate and blend in. Stir till smooth. Leave to cool slightly, or until it begins to thicken a little, but not too much. Put the cake on a rack. Pour chocolate on top of the cake and spread evenly with a large spatula over the top and sides. Shake before it sets to make a smooth surface.

Victoria Sandwich

- Make basic cake mix. Bake in two sandwich tins. Fill centre with 250ml (8fl oz) whipped cream, 3–4 tablespoons jam or flavoured buttercream (see p.163). Dust top with caster sugar.

Madeira cake

- Make basic cake mix, flavouring with the grated zest of a lemon. Bake in one large cake tin. Decorate on top with slice of crystallised lemon.

Lemon Cake

- Make the basic cake mix; flavouring with 1 tablespoon of grated lemon zest. Shortly before the cake is ready, boil 75g (3oz) granulated sugar with the juice of 2 lemons. When the cake comes out of the oven, prick all over the top with a skewer and using a pastry brush, coat the top of the cake with about half the syrup. Leave to cool in the tin. Remove and invert the cake. Prick all over the base and brush with syrup, then brush sides with syrup. Allow to cool before wrapping in clingfilm. Store for 24 hours to allow the syrup to distribute evenly.

Chocolate Loaf

'This is a moist, full-flavoured cake which is shaped in a loaf tin so that slices resemble dark chocolate bread. It needs no icing, but for special occasions it can be coated in chocolate cream icing.'

25g (1oz) best quality cocoa powder

3 tablespoons hot water

3 large eggs, beaten

125g (4½ oz) self-raising cake flour

150g (5½ oz) caster sugar

150g (5½ oz) butter, softened

2 teaspoons vanilla extract

Icing sugar for dusting

Chocolate cream (see p.123) for icing (optional)

- Preheat the oven to 350°F/180°C/Gas 4.
  Line 20 x 10 cm (8 x 4 inch) loaf tin with silicone baking paper, or foil, or greased and floured.

- HEATING THE EGGS: Put eggs, still in their shells, into a bowl of very hot, but not boiling water, leave for 2 minutes to heat the eggs without cooking

- MIXING: Whisk the cocoa powder and hot water together until smooth, then beat in the eggs. Sift flour into a separate large bowl and add caster sugar. Whisk for about 30 seconds using an electric beater. Add all the butter and two thirds of the egg and cocoa mixture to the flour and sugar and beat for about 90 seconds to develop the cake's structure. It should become light and creamy. Scrape down the sides. Add the remaining egg and cocoa mixture, plus the vanilla, and beat for another 30 seconds. Scrape down the sides again and beat for another 30 seconds.

- BAKING: Pour into the prepared tin and bake for 40–50 minutes or until a skewer inserted into the centre of the cake comes out clean and the cake springs back when pressed lightly in the centre. Cool in the tin for 10 minutes and then turn out onto a rack. Dust lightly with icing sugar. Allow to cool before wrapping in clingfilm to store.

Rich and Fudgy Chocolate Cake

'This cake has a fudgy texture and intense chocolate flavour, mellowed by the addition of sour cream. Heavy with butter, it will rise in the oven but flatten on cooling. Best served warm from the oven or reheated, with whipped cream and/or a chocolate sauce.'

40g (1/2 oz) best quality cocoa powder

142ml (5fl oz) carton sour cream or double cream soured with a tablespoon of lemon juice

3 large eggs

1/2 teaspoons vanilla extract

200g (7oz) self-raising cake flour

200g (7oz) caster sugar

200g (7oz) butter, softened

- Preheat the oven to 350°F/180°C/Gas 4. Line or grease with oil and dust with flour or line cake tin 20–23cm (8–9 inch) round cake tin.

- HEATING THE EGGS: Put eggs, still in their shells, into a bowl of very hot, but not boiling water, leave for 2 minutes to heat the eggs without cooking.

- MIXING: Whisk the cocoa powder, sour cream, eggs and vanilla until smooth. Sift flour into a separate large bowl and add caster sugar. Beat with an electric beater for about 30 seconds. Add the butter and two thirds of the egg and cocoa mixture to the flour and beat for about 90 seconds until the mixture comes light and creamy. Scrape down the sides. Add the remaining egg and cocoa mixture in two lots beating for another 20 seconds between each addition.

- BAKING: Pour into the prepared tin and bake for 30–40 minutes or until a skewer inserted into the centre of the cake comes out clean and the cake springs back when pressed in the middle. Cool in the tin for 10 minutes and then turn out onto a rack. Dust lightly with icing sugar.

- SERVING METHOD: From the oven with chocolate sauce (see p.125) and whipped cream or reheated or a few seconds in the microwave.

- Allow to cool before wrapping in clingfilm to store.

Brownies

'This is an excellent recipe which was given to me by Petra Schanhost – a very talented pastry chef from Bremen in Germany, who had worked in Switzerland, London and then with me at One Devonshire.'

375g (13oz) best quality plain chocolate

225g (8oz) unsalted butter

75ml (3fl oz) espresso coffee

225g (8oz) mixed nuts, chopped

4 eggs, beaten

175g (6oz) sugar

125g (4½ oz) plain flour, sifted

- Preheat the oven to 350°F/180°C/Gas 4. Grease with oil, dust with flour or line a rectangular tin approximately 28 x 18cm (11 x 7 inches) and approximately 5cm (2 inches) deep.

- HEATING THE EGGS: Put eggs, still in their shells, into a bowl of very hot, but not boiling water, leave for 2 minutes to heat the eggs without cooking.

- MELTING CHOCOLATE: Put chocolate, butter and espresso into a bowl over a pan of hot water and heat till the chocolate and butter are melted, stirring all the time. Add the nuts.

- MIXING: Break the eggs into the mixing bowl and add the sugar. Beat till white and airy. Stir in the flour gently. Add to the chocolate mixture. Pour into the tin and spread evenly.

- BAKING: Bake for 40–60 minutes. Leave in tin till cold. Cut in squares.

Egg Batter Cakes

This cake method creates the lightest sponges. The technique involves trapping air – created by beating a large amount of eggs with the sugar – so the mixture is extremely delicate and airy and must be treated with care.

It is particularly suitable for sponges which are to be served as desserts, especially with cream. The texture is so delicate that heavy icings such as fondant are unsuitable.

DOS AND DON'TS

- Use only a 'fine' sifted cake flour with no leavening
- Always use caster sugar
- Best results are achieved if eggs are warmed slightly
- Always fold the eggs in very gently with a large metal spoon.
- Work quickly once the eggs are mixed in so that they do not deflate
- Bake immediately after mixing taking care not to knock the tin or shake the mixture
- Allow to cool in the tin before removing
- Keep cooling cake out of draughts

Cream Sponge *(basic cake mix)*

'An everyday family cake, this is a great Scottish favourite, finished with double cream and raspberry or strawberry jam.

When Donald Dewar was visiting One Devonshire as Secretary of State for Scotland he had a couple of slices. His successor, John Reid, also enjoyed this cake.'

6 large eggs
175g (6oz) caster sugar
175g (6oz) plain fine cake flour, sifted

Filling:
300ml (10fl oz) whipped cream
250g (8oz) fresh fruit in season

Preheat the oven to 425°F/220°C/Gas 7. Use 2 x 25cm (10 inch) round cake tins or 3 x 20cm (8 inch) sandwich tins: line with silicone baking paper, or foil, or grease and flour.

HEATING THE EGGS: Put the eggs, still in their shells, into a bowl of very hot, but not boiling water, leave for 2 minutes to heat the eggs without cooking.

MIXING: Put the sugar into the mixing bowl and break in the eggs. Mix at top speed until the mixture turns white and creamy and you can see the trail of the whisk marks in the mix. The mixture should triple in volume. With a large metal spoon, fold in the flour gently, with a cutting and folding movement until all the flour is mixed in. Pour into cake tin(s).

BAKING: Bake for 20–25 minutes. Test for readiness: the top should be golden brown and firm and springy to the touch. Leave to cool in the tin. When cool, remove from the tin, cool on a rack.

FINISHING: Beat cream till stiff and spread half on top of one cake. Cut fruit up finely and place evenly on top. Spread remaining cream on top of fruit. Cover with remaining cake. Dust on top with icing sugar.

Variations on Cream Sponge
Genoese Sponge

'Suitable for a birthday cake or a "designer" cake. I used this recipe for making a "book" cake for the first birthday party of our publisher, Neil Wilson's fiction imprint.'

5 large eggs

2 egg yolks

125g (4½ oz) caster sugar

125g (4½ oz) plain fine cake flour, sifted

25g (1oz) cornflour, sifted with the plain flour

75g (3oz) unsalted butter, melted

Filling/icing:

Classic or Flavoured Buttercream (see p.123)

75g (3oz) chopped nuts (almond, pistachio or hazelnut)

- Preheat the oven to 425°F/220°C/Gas 7. Use 2 x 25cm (10 inch) round cake tins or 3 x 20cm (8 inch) sandwich tins: line with silicone baking paper, or foil, or grease and flour.

- HEATING THE EGGS: Put eggs, still in their shells, into a bowl of very hot, but not boiling water, leave for 2 minutes to heat the eggs without cooking.

- MIXING: Put the sugar into the mixing bowl and break in the eggs. Mix at top speed until the mixture turns white and creamy and you can see the trail of the whisk marks in the mix. The mixture should triple in volume. With a large metal spoon, fold in the flours very gently with a cutting and folding movement until all is mixed in. Dribble the melted butter over the top, a little at a time and fold in carefully. Pour into cake tin(s).

- BAKING: Bake for 20–25 minutes. The top should be golden brown and firm and springy to the touch when it's ready. Leave to cool in the tin. When cool, remove from the tin, and cool on a rack.

- FINISHING: Use whipped cream and fresh fruit as in Cream Sponge (see p.83) or sandwich layers together with classic or flavoured buttercream (see p.122–123). Spread the remaining buttercream smoothly over the top and sides of the cake. Roll the edges in chopped nuts (almonds, pistachios, hazelnuts). Decorate top surface with a fork or knife (or fill a piping bag with buttercream and pipe on top for a more formal decoration).

Chocolate Genoese Sponge

'Soaked in your favourite liqueur syrup, this is a special occasion cake.'

5 large eggs

25g (1oz) best quality cocoa powder, sifted

1 teaspoon vanilla extract

2 tablespoons hot water

125g (4oz) caster sugar

75g (3oz) plain fine cake flour, sifted

3 tablespoons unsalted butter, melted

Coating syrup:

125ml (4fl oz) water

50g (2oz) caster sugar

2 tablespoon liqueur (Drambuie, Glayva or other orange, coffee, hazelnut or raspberry flavoured liqueurs)

Icing and decoration:

Chocolate flavoured buttercream (see p.123)

Chocolate cream icing (see p.123)

125g (4oz) best quality plain chocolate for chocolate scrolls

• Preheat the oven to 425°F/220°C/Gas 7. Use 2 x 25cm (10 inch) round cake tins or three x 20cm (8 inch) sandwich tins: line with silicone baking paper, or foil, or grease and flour.

• HEATING THE EGGS: Put eggs, still in their shells, into a bowl of very hot, but not boiling water, leave for 2 minutes to heat the eggs without cooking.

• MIXING: Put the cocoa powder, vanilla and water into a bowl and mix well. Put the sugar into a separate mixing bowl and break in the eggs. Mix at top speed until the mixture turns white and creamy and you can see the trail of the whisk marks in the mix. The mixture should triple in volume. Remove 2 cups of the egg mixture and mix with the chocolate mixture. Mix till smooth. With a large metal spoon, fold the flour into the remaining egg mixture very gently with a cutting and folding movement until all the flour is mixed in. Then, fold in the chocolate mixture. Dribble the melted butter over the top, a little at a time, folding in carefully. Pour into cake tin.

• BAKING: Bake for 20–25 minutes. The top should be firm and springy to the touch when it's ready. Leave to cool in the tin for 10 minutes. Remove from the tin, and finish cooling on a rack.

• FINISHING: Put sugar and water into a pan, stir to dissolve the sugar and bring to the boil. When all the sugar is dissolved, remove from the heat and leave to cool. Add the liqueur. Soak the cake with the syrup. Sandwich with chocolate buttercream (see p.123). Cover with chocolate cream icing (see p.123).

• DECORATE: To make chocolate scrolls, melt the chocolate in a bowl over a pan of hot water. Very lightly oil the work surface to prevent sticking. Pour out the melted chocolate and spread out thinly. Leave to set. Push a wide-bladed paint-stripper or other similar tool, under the chocolate using a continuous movement which will 'roll' the chocolate. Use to decorate the top of the cake.

Swiss Roll

'The best way to get even baking throughout a swiss roll is to line your trays with foil first and then greaseproof paper.'

Yield: 12-14 slices

75g (3oz) caster sugar

6 egg yolks

3 egg whites

pinch of salt

65g (2½ oz) plain fine cake flour, sifted

15g (½ oz) cornflour, sifted with the flour

Filling:
Jam – 4 tablespoons or 600ml (1pt) soft ice cream or whipped cream

• Preheat the oven to 450°F/230°C/Gas 8. Line a 36 x 25cm (14 x 10inch) swiss roll tin with foil and then greaseproof paper or silicone baking paper.

• MIXING AND BAKING: Put the egg yolks into a mixer bowl and add 1 tablespoon sugar. Put egg whites in separate bowl and beat till they stand up in peaks. Add the remainder of the sugar to the whites in 2–3 lots, beating in between each addition, allowing the whites to thicken. Beat the egg yolks till thick and creamy. Add to the whites and fold in. Sift in flour and cornflour and fold in carefully with a large metal spoon. Pour into prepared tin. Spread evenly. Bake for 10–12 minutes until risen and browned on top.

• FINISHING: While the swiss roll is baking, spread a tea towel on a dry flat surface. Cover with greaseproof paper and dust heavily with caster sugar. Turn out swiss roll onto sugar and peel off paper.

• FILLING WITH JAM: Spread jam while still hot. Make a deep slit half an inch from the end across th bottom edge. Turn in and start to roll up slowly, pulling the towel with it to hold the roll in place. Cut ends to neaten with a sharp knife dipped into a jug of hot water.

• FILLING WITH CREAM OR SOFT ICE CREAM: Place a sheet of paper on top. Make a deep slit half an inch from the end across the bottom edge. Turn in and start to roll up slowly, pulling up the towel with it to hold the roll in place. Cool and then unroll to fill. Re-roll. Keep ice-cream filled swiss roll in the freezer.

Chocolate Swiss Roll

'This can be made as a Yule Log at Christmas with icing and decorations added. Just a thought.'

75gm (3oz) caster sugar

6 egg yolks

3 egg whites

25g (1oz) plain fine cake flour, sifted

40g (1½ oz) best quality cocoa powder, sifted with the flour

15g (½ oz) cornflour, sifted with the flour

- Follow recipe for plain swiss roll adding the cocoa and cornflour with the flour. Fill with chocolate butter cream (see p.123), or 600ml (20fl oz) whipping cream or ice cream.

Torten

'A many-layered cake which comes into the rich and indulgent category.'

4 eggs, separated

125g (4oz) icing sugar

100g (3½ oz) plain fine cake flour

Filling:
Classic buttercream (p.122)

- Preheat the oven to 450°F/230°C/Gas 8. Cut 5 x 18cm (7 inch) rounds of baking parchment or greaseproof paper.

- MIXING: Whisk egg yolks with a tablespoon of icing sugar till stiff. In another bowl beat the egg whites till stiff, adding the remaining icing sugar. Beat till you have a stiff meringue. Add egg yolk mix and whisk in. Add the flour gently, retaining as much air as possible.

- SHAPING and BAKING: Put baking parchment circles on baking trays. Spread the mix evenly over the five rounds. Bake for 7-8 minutes till golden brown.

- FINISHING: Turn over and remove paper. Make buttercream (see p.123). Spread evenly on four rounds and sandwich together. Place fifth round on top. Spread buttercream round sides. Place doily on top. Dust with icing sugar. Remove doily.

Carrot Cake

'This almond and lemon flavoured Swiss carrot cake is quite different to American carrot cake with spices, nuts and dried fruit.'

5 eggs, separated
250g (9oz) carrot, finely grated
300g (10½ oz) ground almonds
75g (3oz) plain fine cake flour, sifted
1 lemon, zest
175g (6oz) soft brown sugar

Topping:
2 tablespoons apricot glaze (see p. 126)
225g (8oz) icing sugar
1–2 tablespoons lemon juice

- Preheat the oven to 350°F/180°C/Gas mark 4. 23–25cm (9–10inch) round cake tin: line with silicone baking paper, or foil, or grease and flour.

- HEATING THE EGGS: Put eggs, still in their shells, into a bowl of very hot, but not boiling water, leave for 2 minutes to heat the eggs without cooking.

- MIXING AND BAKING: Put the carrot, ground almonds, flour and lemon zest into a bowl and mix together. In a clean bowl beat the egg whites and half the sugar, and beat till a thick meringue. Put the yolks with remaining sugar into another bowl and beat till thick and creamy. Add beaten yolks to the carrot mix and mix through gently. Then add the whites and mix till blended. Pour into tin and bake for 45–50 minutes until risen and browned. Cool in tin for ten minutes before turning out onto rack.

- FINISHING: Coat cake lightly with apricot glaze. Leave overnight. Mix icing sugar with lemon juice, adding lemon gradually till thick and spread over cake. Store in an airtight tin.

Sugar Batter Cakes

This is the method which involves creaming the sugar and butter and adding eggs. It creates a close textured, rich sponge which is particularly suitable for heavy fruit cakes.

DOS AND DON'TS

- Use mostly unleavened special cake flour for the finest texture.
- Always use caster sugar.
- All dry ingredients should be at room temperature, eggs and butter slightly warmed.
- If too much egg is added at once and the mixture curdles, add more flour to correct.
- Always beat at the highest mixer speed.
- Cool in the tin for ten minutes before removing to allow the cake to 'set'.

Madeira Cake
(Basic cake mix)

'A few baker's tricks here with white vegetable fat added for a finer crumb and glycerine for a better keeping cake.'

5 eggs

200g (7oz) unsalted butter, softened

75g (3oz) white vegetable fat

200g (7oz) caster sugar

1 teaspoon glycerine

250g (9oz) plain fine cake flour, sifted

50g (2oz) self-raising cake flour

1 teaspoon vanilla extract

1 lemon, grated zest

- Preheat oven to 350°F/180°C/Gas 4. Use a 23–25cm (9–10 inch) round or square cake tin lined with silicone baking paper, or foil, or grease and flour.

- HEATING THE EGGS: Put eggs, still in their shells, into a bowl of very hot, but not boiling water, leave for 2 minutes to heat the eggs without cooking.

- MIXING AND BAKING: Beat the fats and sugar till light and fluffy. Add the glycerine then beat in the eggs in four separate additions, beating well in between. If the mixture curdles, add a little flour and beat in. Fold in remaining flour gently. Add vanilla and lemon zest. Pour into prepared tin and bake for about 60 minutes. Test for readiness when a skewer should come out clean. Cool and store in an airtight tin.

Variations
(*see* variations for vanilla butter sponge p.77)

Sultana Cake

'A traditional Scottish cake that we used to make at all the High Street bakers. You can judge a lazy baker if there are sugar "spots" on the top of his sultana cake, when the mixing and scraping down has been careless. If a job's worth doing, it's worth doing well.'

5 eggs

200g (7oz) unsalted butter, softened

75g (3oz) white vegetable fat

200g (7oz) caster sugar

1 teaspoon glycerine

250g (9oz) plain fine cake flour, sifted

25g (1oz) self-raising cake flour

25g (1oz) ground almonds

1 teaspoon vanilla extract

175g (6oz) sultanas

- Preheat oven to 350°F/180°C/Gas 4. Line with silicone baking paper or foil or grease and flour a round cake tin 23–25cm (9–10 inches).

- HEATING THE EGGS: Put eggs, still in their shells, into a bowl of very hot, but not boiling water. Leave for 2 minutes to heat the eggs without cooking.

- MIXING AND BAKING: Beat the fats and sugar till light and fluffy. Add the glycerine and then the eggs in four separate additions, beating well in between. Fold in flours and ground almonds gently. Add vanilla and sultanas, and mix in. Pour into prepared tin and bake for about 60 minutes. Test for readiness when a skewer should come out clean. Cool and store in an airtight tin.

Dundee Cake

'Though there are many variations of this cake, the original Keiller's "Dundee" cake used only sultanas, almonds, oranges and lemons. The Keiller bakers added some crystallised orange peel from the marmalade production which gave it its special flavour and reputation.'

5 large eggs

250g (9oz) unsalted butter

250g (9oz) caster sugar

300g (10 ½ oz) plain fine cake flour

75g (3oz) ground almonds

1 lemon, zest

1 orange, zest

350g (12oz) sultanas, washed

50g (2oz) crystallised orange peel, finely chopped (or 2 tablespoons thick cut marmalade)

3 tablespoons milk

Topping:
50g (2oz) whole almonds, blanched and halved

- Preheat oven to 350°F/180°C/Gas 4. Line round cake tin 20cm (8 inch) with silicone baking paper or foil.

- HEATING THE EGGS: Put eggs, still in their shells, into a bowl of very hot, but not boiling water. Leave for 2 minutes to heat the eggs without cooking.

- MIXING AND BAKING: Beat the fats and sugar till light and fluffy. Add the eggs in four separate additions, beating well in between. Add a little flour if the mixture curdles and beat well. Gently fold in remaining flour and ground almonds. Add orange and lemon zest, sultanas and orange peel or marmalade. Mix in with milk to dropping consistency. Pour into prepared tin. Cover top with halved blanched almonds and bake for about 1½ hours. Test for readiness when a skewer should come out clean. Cool, wrap and store in an airtight tin.

Robbie Coltrane's Chocolate Cake

'An indulgent, special occasion cake. Certainly not a cake for a weight-watcher's ball. It has a moist, springy sponge, but it's the American frosting, heavy with nuts and coconut, which makes it the real winner – and Coltrane's favourite. I made it for him at One Devonshire.'

4 eggs

125g (4½ oz) best quality plain chocolate

1 teaspoon vanilla extract

125g (4½ oz) unsalted butter

200g (7oz) caster sugar

225g (8oz) plain fine cake flour, sifted with:

1 teaspoon bicarbonate of soda

250ml (9fl oz) buttermilk or fresh milk soured with the juice of a lemon

American Frosting with coconut and pecan nuts:

400ml (14 fl oz) can of evaporated milk

275g (10oz) sugar

125g (4½ oz) butter

4 egg yolks, beaten

1½ teaspoon vanilla extract

200g (7oz) fine coconut

125g (4½ oz) chopped pecan nuts

4 tablespoons apricot jam

- Preheat oven to 350°F/180°C/Gas 4. Line 3 round cake tins 23cm (9 inch).

- HEATING THE EGGS: Put eggs, still in their shells, into a bowl of very hot, but not boiling water, leave for 2 minutes to heat the eggs without cooking.

- MELTING THE CHOCOLATE: Put into a bowl over a pan of hot water and stir till melted. Add vanilla.

- MIXING AND BAKING: Beat the sugar and butter till light and fluffy. Separate the eggs and beat in the yolks one at a time. Add the melted chocolate and vanilla. Beat the egg whites till stiff. Fold the flour and bicarbonate of soda into the cake mixture. Add the buttermilk and finally fold in the egg whites. Bake for 30 minutes till a skewer comes out clean.

- FINISHING: Put the evaporated milk, sugar, butter and egg yolks into a pan and simmer gently, stirring continuously, for about 12 minutes till golden brown and reduced a little. Add the vanilla extract. Add coconut (you can make it fine in a blender) and pecan nuts. Mix through. Spread two layers of the cake with jam and stack the three layers. Cover the top and sides of the cake with the frosting. Rough up with a fork, and leave to harden.

Basic Pastries

These act as a framework, supporting a multitude of different designs, so it's worth making the effort to get the basic structure right. Buying ready-made is the more expensive option but we always made them up in large quantities, which saves both time and money. Things start happening when you master these techniques.

Savoury Short Crust *(basic recipe)*

'This is the simplest pastry to make. I always make it in the mixer since it keeps the pastry cooler, making it less likely to "oil". You can also use a food processor.'

Yield: will fit a 25 x 3.25cm deep (9½ x 1¼ inch) flan ring)

100g (3½ oz) unsalted butter

200g (7oz) plain flour

1-2 tablespoons cold water

Pinch of salt

- MIXING: Put the butter into the mixer bowl (or food processor) and add half the flour. Beat on a slow speed until they have combined into a soft paste. Add remaining flour, salt and 1 tablespoon of water and mix at a slow speed till a smooth firm paste. Add more water if necessary. Do not overmix. Wrap in clingfilm and leave to rest in a cool place for at least an hour before use.

Sweet Short Crust *(basic recipe)*

'An enriched pastry which we used in all sweet flans and tarts.'

Yield: will fit a 25 x 3.25cm deep (9½ x 1¼ inch) flan ring)

100g (3½ oz) unsalted butter

50g (2oz) icing sugar

1 egg yolk

175g (6oz) flour

MIXING: Beat butter and sugar in a mixer (or food processor) till light and fluffy. Add the egg and beat for a minute to mix in, then add the flour and mix on a slow speed till it forms a smooth paste. Do not overmix. Wrap in clingfilm and leave to rest in a cool place for at least an hour or until ready to use.

Frangipan (Almond) Pastry

'This is the rich mixture which we used for filling almond tarts and flans and should not be confused with marzipan for covering cakes.'

Yield: 3.75kg (4 lb)

450g (1lb) unsalted butter

450g (1lb) caster sugar

8 eggs

450g (1lb) ground almonds

125g (4oz) plain flour

1 teaspoon almond extract

MAKING: Beat butter and sugar till white and fluffy. Add eggs, two at a time, beating between each addition. Then add ground almonds, flour and almond essence. Mix till smooth. Store in a sealed container in the fridge, where it will keep for a week. Use as required.

Puff Pastry

'This is the most difficult pastry to make, but gives the most interesting flaky texture and rich buttery flavour. We used it for both sweet and savoury dishes.'

Yield: 1.25kg (2 lb 12oz)

500g (1 lb 2oz) unsalted butter, chilled
500g (1 lb 2oz) strong bread flour
¾ teaspoon sea salt
200ml (7fl oz) water, chilled
30ml (1fl oz) white wine vinegar

- MIXING: Remove 50g (2oz) of the butter and melt. Sieve the flour into a bowl, or onto the table, with the salt. Make a well in the centre and add the melted butter and three-quarters of the water and the vinegar. Bring together into a dough and knead until it is smooth, soft and pliable. Add more water if necessary. Roll into a ball, cut with a cross, cover and leave in a cool place for 2–3 hours.

- ROLLING AND FOLDING: Remove dough from the fridge. Open out the four edges of the cross and place the butter in the centre. Fold the four cut pieces over the butter. Dust with flour and roll out to a square about 70 x 40cm (27 x 16 inches). Fold a third up and a third down. Leave in a cool place to rest for 30 minutes. Give a quarter turn from its original position when it was folded in three and roll out again to the square. Repeat this process twice more with a rest of 30 minutes between each rolling. Cover and refrigerate overnight. Next day give one more rolling and folding. Leave for another 30–60 minutes before use.

- BAKING: Preheat oven to 450°F/230°C/Gas 8

Choux Pastry

'A lot of people are afraid to make this pastry because they have had failures. The secret is not to be in too much of a hurry. Also, don't put it into too hot an oven and never open the door halfway through. It makes a lovely light bun for afternoon teas and desserts.'

100g (3½ oz) unsalted butter
Pinch of salt
Pinch of sugar
250ml (9fl oz) water
150g (5½oz) plain flour
4 large eggs

MIXING AND COOKING: Cut the butter into cubes and put into a pan with the salt, sugar and water. Heat to melt the butter and remove from the heat just before boiling point. Add all the flour and beat vigorously until the mixture thickens. Return to the heat and cut and turn the mixture until it is thoroughly cooked – about 1 minute – when it should leave the sides and base of the pot without sticking. Do not overcook or the pastry will crack when baked.

ADDING EGGS: Put the mixture into a bowl and continue to cut and turn it for a minute. Add the eggs, one at a time, beating between each addition (if using mixer on speed 3–4). Cover and keep in a cool place till ready for use. *See* recipes for eclairs, choux buns and profiteroles (see p.115).

Savoury Pastries

All these recipes combine a pastry with a savoury filling. At One Devonshire we made quiches in 10–12 portion sizes. While they may be large for everyday meals, they will keep for at least a week in the fridge, making useful 'stand by' meals. Quiches are great party and buffet dishes, the sausage rolls and bridies are versatile as picnic or high tea items. A steak pie is the traditional Scottish family-round-the-table meal made to perfection by many high street butchers.

Quiche Lorraine

'You will find most British versions finish this quiche with grated cheese though the correct Lorraine quiche has no such addition. At the end of the day, though, it's a matter of taste. I prefer to add the cheese.'

Yield: 12 from 25 x 3.25cm deep (9¾ x 1¼ inch deep) flan tin with removeable base.

Savoury short crust pastry:

100g (3½ oz) unsalted butter
200g (7oz) plain flour
1–2 tablespoons water
Pinch of salt

Filling:
2 tablespoons oil
1 onion, finely chopped
150g (5oz) bacon, finely diced
250ml (8fl oz) single cream
250ml (8fl oz) milk
4 large eggs
4 egg yolks
Salt and pepper
75g (3oz) mature cheddar, finely grated
Beaten egg for brushing

- Preheat the oven to 350°F/180°C/Gas 4. Grease flan tin.

- MAKING THE PASTRY: Put the butter into the mixer bowl (or food processor) and add half the flour. Beat on a slow speed until this has come together into a soft paste. Add remaining flour, salt and 1 tablespoon water and mix at a slow speed till a smooth paste. Add more water if necessary. The less water the shorter the pastry. Do not overmix. Wrap in clingfilm and leave to rest in a cool place for at least an hour before use.

- MAKING THE FILLING: Heat the oil in a frying pan and sauté the onions and bacon for about 4 minutes till lightly cooked but not browned. Put into a dish and leave to cool. Meanwhile put the cream, milk, salt, pepper and eggs into the mixer bowl and beat on slow till the eggs are mixed in. Strain.

- LINING FLAN, BAKING BLIND. Roll out the chilled pastry on a lightly floured work surface to a circle large enough to fill the base and sides of the flan tin plus about 1cm (½ inch). Lift over rolling pin into the flan tin and press into the base and sides. Do not cut off the overhang. Place a sheet of foil in the base, pressing the foil into the corners and up the sides. Fill with dry beans or rice. Bake blind for 18–20 minutes or until pastry is set. Remove from the oven, take out foil and beans. Brush the base and sides with a little beaten egg and return to the oven to dry out for another 10 minutes. The pastry should be crisp. With a sharp knife remove excess pastry from the edge.

- FINISHING THE QUICHE: Put the bacon and onions in the base and add a little of the milk and eggs mixture. Spread evenly. Put onto baking tray and place in the oven. Fill up with the rest of the liquid while inside the oven. Sprinkle the top with cheese. Bake for about 1 hour till firm on top. Serve hot or cold. If to be cut in portions, cut before it cools, otherwise the crisp pastry may splinter.

Spinach Quiche

'This has a lovely rich green colour and an intense flavour.'

Yield: 12 slices from 25 x 3.25cm deep (9¾ x 1¼ inch deep) flan tin with removeable base.

Savoury short crust pastry:
100g (3½ oz) unsalted butter
200g (7oz) plain flour
1–2 tablespoons water
Pinch of salt

Filling:
2 tablespoons oil
1 onion, finely chopped
350g (12oz) fresh young spinach, finely chopped
25g (1oz) butter
150ml (5fl oz) single cream
3 large eggs
3 egg yolks
Salt and pepper
100g (4oz) mature cheddar, finely grated
Beaten egg for brushing base of pastry case

- Preheat the oven to 350°F/180°C/Gas 4. Grease flan tin.

- MAKING THE PASTRY: Put the butter into the mixer bowl (or food processor) and add half the flour. Beat on a slow speed until this comes together into a soft paste. Add remaining flour, salt and water and mix at a slow speed till a smooth paste. Do not overmix. Wrap in clingfilm and leave to rest in a cool place for at least an hour before use.

- MAKING THE FILLING: Heat the oil in a frying pan and sauté the onions till soft and transparent. Add the spinach and butter and sauté lightly till the spinach wilts. Leave to cool a little. Meanwhile put the cream, eggs and half the cheese into a bowl and whisk together.

- LINING FLAN, BAKING BLIND. Roll out the chilled pastry on a lightly floured work surface to a circle large enough to fill the base and sides of the flan tin plus about 1cm (½ inch) extra. Lift over rolling pin into the flan tin and press into the base and sides. Do not cut off the overhang. Place a sheet of foil in the base, pressing the foil into the corners and up the sides. Fill with dry beans or rice. Bake blind for 18–20 minutes or until pastry is set. Remove from the oven, take out foil and beans. Brush the base and sides with a little beaten egg and return to the oven to dry out for another 10 minutes or until the pastry is crisp. With a sharp knife remove excess pastry from the edge.

- FINISHING THE QUICHE: Put flan on a baking sheet. For a fine texture (optional) put the spinach and onion mix into the food processor and blend till fairly fine, but not too fine. Mix spinach with cheese and egg mixture, add salt and pepper, and pour into flan case. Sprinkle the rest of the cheese on top. Bake for about 45–60 minutes till firm and lightly browned on top. Serve hot or cold. If to be cut in portions, cut before it cools, otherwise the crisp pastry will splinter.

Sausage Rolls

'These are quick and easy to make with ready-made puff pastry. A big difference from those you buy. I know which I would go for.'

Yield: 12–18

400g (14oz) puff pastry (see p.94)
200g (7oz) sausage meat
Beaten egg for glazing

- Preheat oven to 450°F/230°C/Gas 8. Greased baking tray.

- SHAPING: Roll out the pastry on a cool, floured surface to a square about 5mm (¼ inch) thick. Trim edges and cut in half lengthways. There are now two rectangles. Brush off excess flour and brush surface with egg. Roll out sausage into two strips to fit the two pastry rectangles and lay in the middle of the pastry. Fold over pastry and seal edges together firmly. Trim edge. Criss-cross a design with back of a knife. Brush with beaten egg. Cut into approximately 6cm (3 inch) lengths. Bake for about 20 minutes till risen and browned. Serve hot.

- *Note*: this is the French style of sausage roll. For an English style sausage roll: the pastry is rolled round the sausage with the edges overlapping so the cooking time is slightly longer.

Bridies

'Though traditional Forfar Bridies are always made with short pastry, Glasgow bakers all make theirs with puff and call them "bridies".'

Yield: 7–8

2 tablespoons oil
1 large onion, finely chopped
250g (9oz) steak mince
Salt and pepper
200g (7oz) puff pastry (see p.94)
Beaten egg for brushing

- Preheat the oven to 450°F/230°C/Gas 8. Greased baking tray.

- MAKING FILLING: Heat the oil in a frying pan and add the onion. Cook gently till softened without browning. Remove from the pan and put into a bowl. Add the mince and cook until lightly browned. Put into the bowl with the onions and season with salt and pepper.

- SHAPING AND BAKING: Roll out the pastry to about 1cm (½ inch) thick and cut into 7.5mm (3 inch) rounds. Roll out into oval shapes until they're about 5mm (¼ inch) thick. Place a spoonful of the mince and onions in the middle. Wet edges and seal to make a semi-circular oval shape. Make a small hole in the top. Brush with beaten egg and bake in a very hot oven for about 10–15 minutes till golden brown and risen. Serve hot.

Steak and Kidney Pie

'This is the traditional pie served in Scotland for New Year's dinner. The kidney filling is the up-market version, sausages are a cheaper option. Bakers and butchers who make these pies, will always cook the steak before making the pie. This is necessary only if the less tender cuts of stewing steak are being used.'

Yield: 4–6

200g (7oz) puff pastry

2 tablespoons oil

1 large onion, finely chopped

500g (1lb) best stewing steak

250g (8oz) kidney or sausages

1 tablespoon plain flour seasoned with salt and pepper

Water or stock

Salt

Freshly ground black pepper

1 beaten egg for brushing

- Preheat the oven to 450°F/230°C/Gas 8. Use a 1L (2pt) pie dish and pie funnel or small cup.

- PREPARING THE PASTRY LID: Roll out the pastry till it's about 2.5cm (1 inch) larger than the rim of the pie dish. Invert the pie dish and place on top of the pastry. Cut round the edge of the pie dish. Wet pie dish rim. Cut the excess pastry into a long strip the width of the pie dish edge and place on rim. Press down well. Wet the edges of the strip. Reserve the leftover pastry to make 'leaves'.

- MAKING THE FILLING: Heat the oil in a pan and add the onion. Sauté till well browned but not burnt. Beat the steak with a rolling pin and cut into thin strips. Skin, split and remove the core of the kidney. (Grill or fry sausages.) Toss the steak and kidney in flour and mix with the onions. Put into the pie dish and place pie funnel or cup in the centre. Pour in enough water or stock to come halfway up the filling.

- FINISHING AND BAKING: Place on lid and press down well to seal. Cut any leftover pastry into 'leaves' (see p.138). Make a small hole in the centre of the pastry and brush the surface lightly with beaten egg. Place on pastry 'leaves'. Brush with egg. Leave to rest for half an hour. Brush again lightly with beaten egg. Bake in a hot oven till the pastry is risen and light brown. Turn down to 350°F/180°C/Gas 4 and bake for another hour until the steak is cooked. If the pastry begins to darken too much, cover with a sheet of foil. Fill up, through hole in the lid, with a little hot stock or water if necessary before serving.

Pastry Desserts

All these recipes bring together a pastry and a filling. They are therefore quite time consuming – except perhaps the apple pie and the jam tarts – which makes most of them special occasion rather than everyday desserts.

At One Devonshire we made all the flans and tarts in 12 portions, since the same time and effort goes into this as into a 4 portion tart. While they are always at their best just after they've been made, most keep well for a few days and some can be frozen in individual portions.

Apple Pie

'A classic pudding. In autumn, brambles (blackberries) can be added.'

Yield: 4-6

Sweet shortcrust pastry:
100g (3½ oz) unsalted butter
50g (2oz) icing sugar
1 egg yolk
175g (6oz) plain flour

Filling:
1kg (2lb 4oz) tart cooking apples
100g (4oz) soft brown sugar
1 teaspoon cinnamon or mixed spice
1 lemon, juice and zest

Dredging:
caster sugar

- Preheat the oven to 350°F/180°C/Gas 4. Use a 1L (2pt) deep pie dish.

- MAKING THE PASTRY: Beat butter and sugar in a mixer (or blend in a food processor) till light and fluffy. Add the egg and beat for a minute to mix in. Add the flour and mix on a slow speed till it forms a smooth paste. Do not overmix. Wrap in clingfilm and leave to rest for at least an hour in a cool place till ready to use.

- MAKING THE PIE AND BAKING: Roll out the pastry about 2.5cm (1 inch) larger than the rim of the pie dish. Invert pie dish and place on top of pastry. Cut round to fit. Wet pie dish rim. Cut the excess pastry into a long strip and place on rim. Press down well. Wet edges. Peel, core and slice the apples. Mix the sugar and cinnamon. Put apples into the pie dish in layers, sprinkling with lemon juice and zest and the spiced sugar. They should be heaped well above the rim of the pie dish. Place on lid and press down well to seal. Make a small hole in the centre for the steam to escape. Pinch the edge to make a decorative finish, or mark with a fork. Bake for 40–50 minutes till apples are cooked. Cover pastry with foil if it darkens too much. Dredge with caster sugar and serve hot or cold with cream or custard.

Lemon Meringue Pie

'A triumph of textures in crisp pastry, soft lemony filling and marshmallowy meringue.'

Yield: 12 from 25 x 3.25cm deep
(9¾ x 1¼ inch deep) flan tin with removeable base.

Pastry:
100g (3½ oz) unsalted butter
50g (2oz) icing sugar
1 egg yolk
175g (6oz) plain flour
Beaten egg for brushing

Filling:
125g (4oz) sugar
25g (1oz) cornflour
4 lemons, zest and juice
6 egg yolks
50g (2oz) butter
200ml (7fl oz) milk
2-3 tablespoons single cream

Meringue:
6 egg whites
Pinch of salt
200g (6oz) caster sugar

- Preheat the oven to 350°F/180°C/Gas 4 then turn down to 300°F/140°C/Gas 2.
  Grease flan tin.

- MAKING PASTRY: Beat butter and sugar in a mixer (or blend in a food processor) till light and fluffy. Add the eggs and beat for a minute to mix in. Add the flour and mix on a slow speed until it forms a smooth paste. Do not overmix. Wrap in clingfilm and leave to rest in a cool place for at least an hour before use.

- LINING FLAN, BAKING BLIND: Roll out on a lightly floured work surface to a circle large enough to fill the base and sides of the flan tin plus about 1cm (½ inch) extra. Lift over rolling pin into the flan tin and press into the base and sides. Do not cut off the overhang. Place a sheet of foil in the base, pressing the foil into the corners and up the sides. Fill with dry beans or rice. Bake blind for 18–20 minutes or until pastry is set. Remove from the oven, take out foil and beans. Brush the base and sides with a little beaten egg and return to the oven to dry out for another 10 minutes or until crisp. Trim off surplus pastry with a sharp knife.

- MAKING THE FILLING: Put the sugar, cornflour, lemon juice and yolks into a bowl and beat together till the sugar is dissolved. Heat the milk, butter and lemon zest in a pan and slowly bring almost to the boil. Leave to infuse for five minutes. Strain over the egg mixture whisking all the time. Return to the pan and cook slowly over a low heat, stirring all the time, until the custard has thickened. Add cream to thin down a little. Pour into prepared flan tin.

- MAKING THE MERINGUE: Whisk egg whites and salt till they form peaks and then add about half the sugar gradually in tablespoons, beating between each addition. Stir in remaining sugar gradually and when mixed in, pipe on or pile on top of filling. Dust with caster sugar on top to give a crisp finish.

- BAKING: Bake at the cooler temperature till lightly browned for about 30–40 minutes.

Lemon Tart

'This is the Rolls Royce of tarts. Intensely sharp lemon is balanced with rich eggs, butter and sugar. For special occasions.'

Yield: 12 from 25 x 3.25cm deep (9¾ x 1¼ inch deep) flan tin with removeable base

Pastry:

100g (3½ oz) unsalted butter

50g (2oz) icing sugar

1 egg yolk

175g (6oz) plain flour

Beaten egg for brushing base

Filling:

8 eggs

275g (9½ oz) caster sugar

250ml (9fl oz) lemon juice

(approximately 4–5 lemons)

1 tablespoon grated lemon zest

150ml (5fl oz) double cream

Optional: substitute one orange for a lemon

- Preheat the oven to 350°F/180°C/Gas 4. Grease flan tin.

- MAKING FILLING and BAKING: Break the eggs into a bowl, beat lightly and add the sugar and lemon juice and zest. Continue to beat lightly till sugar is dissolved. Pour 3–4 tablespoons of the egg mixture into the cream and mix till blended. Transfer into the egg mixture and blend together. Put into a large jug and place in the fridge. Leave overnight or for several hours, until any froth subsides.

- MAKING PASTRY AND BAKING FLAN: Beat butter and sugar in a mixer (or blend in a food processor) till light and fluffy. Add the egg and beat for a minute to mix in. Add the flour and mix on a slow speed until it forms a smooth paste. Do not overmix. Wrap in clingfilm and leave to rest in a cool place for at least an hour before use.

- LINING FLAN, BAKING BLIND: Roll out on a lightly floured work surface to a circle large enough to fill the base and sides of the flan tin plus about 1cm (½ inch). Lift over rolling pin into the flan tin and press into the base and sides. Do not cut off the overhang. Place a sheet of foil in the base, pressing the foil into the corners and up the sides. Fill with dry beans or rice. Bake blind for 18–20 minutes or until pastry is set. Remove from the oven, take out foil and beans. Brush the base and sides with a little beaten egg and return to the oven to dry out for another 10 minutes. The pastry should be crisp. Trim off surplus pastry with a sharp knife.

- BAKING: Turn down oven to 325°F/ 170°C°/Gas 3. Put flan in the oven and pour in mixture. Bake slowly for 30 minutes at 325°F/170°C/ Gas 3 or until set. The middle should be just set. Dust with icing sugar when it comes out of the oven and caramelise under a hot grill or with a pastry blowtorch. If to be cut in portions, cut before it cools otherwise the crisp pastry may splinter.

Chocolate Tart

'We served this fantastic tart at the Triangle.'

Yield: 12 from 25 x 3.25cm deep (9¾ x 1¼ inch deep) flan tin with removeable base.

Pastry:
100g (3½ oz) unsalted butter
50g (2oz) icing sugar
1 egg yolk
175g (6oz) plain flour
Beaten egg for brushing the base

Filling:
350g (12oz) best quality plain chocolate
125g (4½ oz) unsalted butter
4 eggs
25g (1oz) caster sugar*

Icing sugar for dusting
Serve with whipped cream or crème fraiche

*　The amount of sugar can be increased, this depends on taste and the bitterness of the plain chocolate.

- Preheat the oven to 425°F/220°C/Gas 7. Grease flan tin.

- MAKING PASTRY AND BAKING FLAN: Beat butter and sugar in a mixer (or blend in a food processor) till light and fluffy. Add the egg and beat for a minute to mix in. Add the flour and mix on a slow speed until it forms a smooth paste. Do not overmix. Wrap in clingfilm and leave to rest in a cool place for at least an hour before use.

- LINING FLAN, BAKING BLIND. Roll out on a lightly floured work surface to a circle large enough to fill the base and sides of the flan tin plus about 1cm (½ inch) overhang. Lift over rolling pin into the flan tin and press into the base and sides. Do not cut off the overhang. Place a sheet of foil in the base, pressing the foil into the corners and up the sides. Fill with dry beans or rice. Bake blind for 18–20 minutes or until pastry is set. Remove from the oven, take out foil and beans. Brush the base and sides with a little beaten egg and return to the oven to dry out for another 10 minutes. The pastry on the base should be crisp. Trim off surplus pastry with a sharp knife.

- MAKING FILLING and BAKING: Break up the chocolate and place in a bowl over simmering water. Add the butter, heat until the chocolate and butter are melted. Remove from the heat and leave to cool a little. Meanwhile whisk the eggs and sugar over hot water until they are beginning to thicken and turn creamy. Do not overbeat. If too much air is beaten in to the mixture at this stage it will not fit the flan. When the chocolate is hand hot, fold in half the beaten egg mixture. Fold in remainder of egg mixture and when evenly mixed pour into flan. It should come about three-quarters of the way up the sides. Bake until the mixture is just set and firm on top. About 10 minutes. Dust on top with icing sugar. Serve lukewarm, with whipped cream or crème fraiche. If to be cut in portions, cut before it cools since the crisp pastry may splinter.

Bakewell Tart

'A good afternoon tea tart.'

Yield: 12 from 25 x 3.25cm deep (9¾ x 1¼ inch deep) flan tin with removeable base.

Pastry:
100g (3½ oz) unsalted butter
50g (2oz) icing sugar
1 egg yolk
175g (6oz) plain flour

Filling:
225g (8oz) caster sugar
225g (8oz) butter
4 large eggs
225g (8oz) ground almonds
1 tablespoon plain flour, sifted
1 teaspoon almond extract
2 tablespoons raspberry jam

Dusting:
icing sugar

- Preheat the oven to 375°F/190°C/Gas 5. Grease flan tin.

- MAKING THE PASTRY AND LINING THE FLAN: Beat butter and sugar in a mixer (or blend in a food processor) till light and fluffy. Add the egg and beat for a minute to mix in. Add the flour and mix on a slow speed until it forms a smooth paste. Do not overmix. Wrap in clingfilm and leave to rest in a cool place for at least an hour before use. Roll out to about 5mm (¼ inch) and line flan tin.

- HEATING THE EGGS: Put eggs, still in their shells, into a bowl of very hot, but not boiling water, leave for 2 minutes to heat the eggs without cooking.

- MAKING THE FILLING AND BAKING: Beat the sugar and butter till light and fluffy. Add the eggs, one at a time, beating well between each addition. Fold in the almonds and flour and stir in the almond extract. Spread the jam evenly in the base of the flan tin. Add the filling and spread over evenly. Bake for about 20–30 minutes till risen and golden brown. Dust lightly with icing sugar before serving.

Apple and Almond Tart

'A showy tart with thinly sliced apples making the decoration on top of an intense almond flavoured filling.'

Yield: 12 from 25 x 3.25cm deep (9¼ x 1¼ inch deep) flan tin with removeable base.

12 well-flavoured eating apples

2 tablespoons water

3–4 cloves

2 sticks cinnamon

Pastry:

100g (3½ oz) unsalted butter

50g (2oz) icing sugar

2 eggs

1 egg yolk

175g (6oz) plain flour

Frangipan filling:

100g (4oz) unsalted butter

100g (4oz) icing sugar

100g (4oz) ground almonds

25g (1oz) plain flour

2 eggs

2 teaspoons almond extract

2 tablespoons melted butter for brushing apples

2 tablespoons apricot jam for glazing

- Preheat the oven to 375°F/190°C/Gas 5. Grease flan tin.

- COOKING THE APPLES: Peel, core and slice 6 apples. Place in a pan with a few tablespoons of water and the spices and stew till soft. Cool.

- MAKING THE PASTRY AND BAKING THE FLAN: Beat butter and sugar in a mixer (or blend in a food processor) till light and fluffy. Add the egg and beat for a minute to mix in. Add the flour and mix on a slow speed until it forms a smooth paste. Do not overmix. Wrap in clingfilm and leave to rest in a cool place for at least an hour before use. Roll out on a lightly floured work surface to a circle large enough to fill the flan tin. Lift over rolling pin into the flan tin and press into the base and sides. Leave to rest for ½ hour and trim edges.

- HEATING THE EGGS: Put eggs, still in their shells, into a bowl of very hot, but not boiling water, leave for 2 minutes to heat the eggs without cooking.

- FILLING AND BAKING: Make the filling by beating the butter and icing sugar till fluffy. Add the eggs, one at a time. Beat well and then add the ground almonds and flour. Mix in the almond extract. Beat for a few minutes on a high speed to lighten the mixture. Spread the stewed apples on the base of the flan and cover with the frangipan mixture. Spread evenly. Peel the remaining apples. Cut in half and remove the cores with a small sharp knife. Place each half apple cut side down, and slice thinly, keeping the shape of the halves. Push gently with the palm of your hand to spread out the apple slices and lift each half apple on a pallet knife on top of the frangipan. Begin at the centre working outwards to make a pattern. Press each line of apple slices gently into the frangipan. Brush liberally with butter. Bake for about 50 minutes till firm and lightly browned on top.

- FINISHING: Melt apricot jam, sieve and brush over the top to give a glaze. Serve hot or cold.

Plum Tart

'This is a French tart filled with pastry cream and cooked fruit in season, finished on top with a glaze. It is a useful tart for making ahead.'

Yield: 12 from 25 x 3.25cm deep (9¾ x 1¼ inch deep) flan tin with removeable base.

Pastry:

100g (3½ oz) unsalted butter

50g (2oz) icing sugar

1 egg yolk

175g (6oz) plain flour

Beaten egg for brushing

Pastry cream (*crème patisserie*) see p.122:

300ml (10fl oz) milk

1 teaspoon vanilla extract or 1 vanilla pod

100g (3oz) caster sugar

6 egg yolks

25g (1oz) plain flour

25g (1oz) cornflour

100ml (3½ fl oz) whipping cream, whipped

Filling:

15 Victoria plums (or other plums, greengages or damsons)

4 tablespoons cold water

4 tablespoons caster sugar

2 tablespoons of apricot jam for glaze

- Preheat the oven to 375°F/190°C/Gas 5. Grease flan tin.

- MAKING PASTRY: Beat butter and sugar in a mixer (or blend in a food processor) till light and fluffy. Add the egg and beat for a minute to mix in. Add the flour and mix on a slow speed until it forms a smooth paste. Do not overmix. Wrap in clingfilm and leave to rest for at least an hour in a cool place till ready to use.

- LINING FLAN: Roll out on a lightly floured work surface to a circle large enough to fill the base and sides of the flan tin plus about 1cm (½ inch) extra. Lift over rolling pin into the flan tin and press into the base and sides. Trim off the overhang.

- TO MAKE: Put the milk into a pan and bring to the boil. If using a vanilla pod scrape out the seeds and add pod and seeds to milk. Leave to infuse for at least ten minutes. Strain. Beat the egg yolks and sugar together till thick and creamy. Sift in the flour and cornflour. Add vanilla extract if using. Pour the heated milk over gradually, beating all the time. Return to the pan and heat gently stirring all the time with a wooden spoon. Once it begins to thicken, beat vigorously till it comes to a smooth thickened paste. Cook for a few minutes, then leave to cool. Beat in whipped cream and spread evenly over pastry.

- PREPARING THE PLUMS AND BAKING: Wash the fruit and cut in half. Remove stones. Place face down on a baking tin. Sprinkle with water and sugar and bake for 10–15 minutes to soften a little. Drain plums, reserving the juice and neatly place on top of pastry cream. Bake for about 40-60 minutes or until tart is cooked.

- FINISHING: Boil apricot jam with the plum juice and reduce to a smooth glaze. Brush all over tart and leave to cool. Serve at room temperature.

Clafoutis Tart

'A French summer tart which is made when cherries are plentiful, it can also be made with other fruits or, as in this version, with prunes.'

Yield: 12 from 25 x 3.25cm deep (9¾ x 1¼ inch deep) flan tin with removeable base

Pastry:

100g (3½ oz) unsalted butter

50g (2oz) icing sugar

1 egg yolk

175g (6oz) plain flour

Filling:

12 stoned and soaked prunes, cut into 4

2-3 teaspoons Armagnac

125ml (4fl oz) fresh milk

125ml (4fl oz) double cream

4 eggs

75g (3oz) caster sugar

15g (½ oz) plain flour

• Preheat the oven to 375°F/190°C/Gas 5. Grease flan tin.

• MAKING THE PASTRY: Beat butter and sugar in a mixer (or blend in a food processor) till light and fluffy. Add the egg and beat for a minute to mix in. Add the flour and mix on a slow speed until it forms a smooth paste. Do not overmix. Wrap in clingfilm and leave to rest in a cool place for at least an hour till ready to use.

• LINING FLAN, BAKING BLIND: Roll out on a lightly floured work surface to a circle large enough to fill the base and sides of the flan tin plus about 1cm (½ inch). Lift over rolling pin into the flan tin and press into the base and sides. Do not cut off the overhang. Place a sheet of foil in the base, pressing the foil into the corners and up the sides. Fill with dry beans or rice. Bake blind for 18–20 minutes or until pastry is set. Remove from the oven, take out foil and beans. Brush the base and sides with a little beaten egg and return to the oven to dry out for another 10 minutes. The pastry should be crisp. Trim off edges with a sharp knife. Put prunes evenly over the base. Sprinkle over Armagnac.

• MAKING THE FILLING: Put the cream and milk into a pan and bring to the boil. Whisk the eggs and sugar in a bowl until they begin to thicken and turn creamy. Do not overbeat or the mixture will not fit the flan. Add the milk mixture. Stir gently. Fold in the flour to make a smooth batter. Half fill the pastry shell and put into the oven. Put the remaining mixture into a jug and pour into the tart.

• BAKING: Bake till risen and set, about 50 minutes. Remove and dust with granulated sugar. Serve warm with whipped cream.

Macaroon Tart

'This is a simple tart to make, suitable for afternoon tea.'

Yield: 12 slices from 25 x 3.25cm deep (9¾ x 1¼inch deep) flan tin with removeable base.

Pastry:

100g (3½ oz) unsalted butter

50g (2 oz) icing sugar

1 egg yolk

175g (6oz) plain flour

Beaten egg

Filling:

125g (4½ oz) caster sugar

100g (3½ oz) ground almonds

3 egg whites

1 teaspoon lemon juice

2–3 tablespoons raspberry jam

- Preheat the oven to 375°F/190°C/Gas 5. Grease flan tin.

- MAKING THE PASTRY: Beat butter and sugar in a mixer (or blend in a food processor) till light and fluffy. Add the eggs and beat for a minute to mix in. Add the flour and mix on a slow speed until it forms a smooth paste. Do not overmix. Wrap in clingfilm and leave to rest in a cool place for at least an hour before use. Roll out to about 0.5cm (¼ inch) on a floured board and line flan tin. Trim off excess pastry with a sharp knife.

- MAKING FILLING AND BAKING: Mix the sugar and almonds together in a bowl. Put lemon juice into the egg whites and beat till stiff. Put into the bowl with sugar and almonds and fold gently together. Spread flan with jam. Pour filling into flan tin and spread evenly. Bake for 30 minutes till risen and browned.

Cheesecake

'Italian ricotta or full fat soft cheese makes the richest cheesecake, though a lighter version can also be made with soft cream cheese with a low fat content.'

Yield: 12 slices from 25 x 3.25cm deep (9¾ x 1¼ inch deep) flan tin with removeable base

Pastry:
100g (3½ oz) unsalted butter
50g (2oz) icing sugar
1 egg yolk
175g (6oz) plain flour

Beaten egg for brushing

Filling:
600g (1lb 5oz) ricotta, or low fat soft cheese
50g (2oz) caster sugar
4 egg yolks
1 tablespoon grated orange or lemon zest
2 teaspoon plain flour
25g (1oz) California raisins

- Preheat the oven to 350°F/180°C/Gas 4. Grease flan tin.

- MAKING PASTRY AND BAKING FLAN: Beat butter and sugar in a mixer (or blend in a food processor) till light and fluffy. Add the egg and beat for a minute to mix in. Add the flour and mix on a slow speed until it forms a smooth paste. Do not overmix. Wrap in clingfilm and leave to rest in a cool place for at least an hour before use.

- LINING FLAN, BAKING BLIND: Roll out on a lightly floured work surface to a circle large enough to fill the base and sides of the flan tin plus about 1cm (½ inch). Lift over rolling pin into the flan tin and press into the base and sides. Do not cut off the overhang. Place a sheet of foil in the base, pressing the foil into the corners and up the sides. Fill with dry beans or rice. Bake blind for 18–20 minutes or until pastry is set. Remove from the oven, take out foil and beans. Brush the base and sides with a little beaten egg and return to the oven to dry out for another 10 minutes. The pastry should be crisp. Trim off overhang with a sharp knife.

- MAKING FILLING AND BAKING: Put the cheese, sugar, egg yolks, orange or lemon zest into a bowl and beat till light and creamy. Mix in flour and raisins. Pour into flan. Bake for about 25–30 minutes till firm and set on top. Leave to cool. Remove sides of flan tin leaving cheesecake on the base. Serve cold.

Fresh Fruit Flan

'This is another French tart which has endless possibilities, depending on the fruit in season.'

Yield: 12 from 25 x 3.25cm deep (9¾ x 1¼ inch deep) flan tin with removeable base.

Pastry:
100g (3½ oz) unsalted butter

50g (2oz) icing sugar

1 egg yolk

175g (6oz) plain flour

Beaten egg for brushing

Pastry cream (crème patisserie see p. 122):
300ml (10fl oz) milk

1 teaspoon vanilla extract or 1 vanilla pod

75g (3oz) caster sugar

6 egg yolks

25g (1oz) plain flour

25g (1oz) cornflour

100ml (3½ fl oz) whipping cream, whipped

Filling:
Approximately 750g (1½ lb) fruit in season

200g (7oz) raspberries

200g (7oz) strawberries

1 bunch black or green grapes

Dusting:
50g (2oz) icing sugar

15g (½oz) cornflour

- Preheat the oven to 350°F/180°C/Gas 4. Grease flan tin.

- MAKING PASTRY AND BAKING FLAN: Beat butter and sugar in a mixer till light and fluffy. Add the egg and beat for a minute to mix in. Add the flour and mix on a slow speed until it forms a smooth paste. Do not overmix. Wrap in clingfilm and leave to rest in a cool place for at least an hour before use.

- LINING FLAN, BAKING BLIND: Roll out, on a lightly floured work surface, to a circle large enough to fill the base and sides of the flan tin plus about 1cm (½ inch). Lift over rolling pin into the flan tin and press into the base and sides. Do not cut off the overhang. Place a sheet of foil in the base, pressing the foil into the corners and up the sides. Fill with dry beans or rice. Bake blind for 18–20 minutes or until pastry is set. Remove from the oven, take out foil and beans. Brush the base and sides with a little beaten egg and return to the oven to dry out for another 10 minutes. The pastry should be crisp. Trim off overhang with a sharp knife.

- TO MAKE: Put the milk into a pan and bring to the boil. If using a vanilla pod scrape out seeds and add pod and seeds to milk. Leave to infuse for at least ten minutes. Strain. Beat the egg yolks and sugar together till thick and creamy. Sift in the flour and cornflour. Pour the heated milk over gradually, beating all the time. Return to the pan and heat gently stirring all the time with a wooden spoon. Once it begins to thicken, beat vigorously till it comes to a smooth thickened paste. Cook for a few minutes. Add vanilla extract if using and beat in. Cool.

- FINISHING THE FLAN: Clean the fruit, if necessary. Mix the crème patisserie with the cream to make a fairly firm mixture. Fill flan and lay fruit on top. Dust with icing sugar mixed with a little cornflour (the cornflour prevents the sugar dissolving). Cut in slices and serve.

Spiced Apple Turnovers

Yield: 24

8 cooking apples

4 tablespoons water

3-4 cloves

200 g (7oz) puff pastry (see p.94)

25g (1oz) ground almonds

75g (3oz) sultanas

2 egg whites for brushing

100g (3½ oz) sugar for dusting

- Preheat the oven to 425°F/220°C/Gas 7. Greased baking tray.

- PREPARING THE APPLES: Peel, core and slice the apples. Put in a pan with water and cloves. Simmer till the apples are soft. Drain, mash and leave to cool.

- SHAPING AND BAKING: Roll out the pastry to about 5mm (¼ inch) and cut in rounds 6cm (2½ inch). Roll out into slightly thinner oval shapes and cut a hole in the top half with the end of an apple corer or plastic tube. Brush pastry with cold water. Mix the apples with the ground almonds and sultanas and place in spoonfuls on the half of the pastry without the hole. Fold over and seal round the edges. Brush with egg white and dust with caster sugar. Bake for 15—20 minutes till risen and golden brown.

Jam Tarts

Yield: 14–18

Pastry:

100g (3½ oz) unsalted butter

50g (2oz) icing sugar

1 egg

175g (6oz) plain flour

Filling:

150g (5oz) home-made or high-fruit commercial jam

- Preheat the oven to 375°F/190°C/Gas 5. Grease 14–18 x 5cm (2inch) tartlet cases.

- MAKING THE PASTRY: Beat butter and sugar in a mixer (or blend in a food processor) till light and fluffy. Add the egg and beat for a minute to mix in. Add the flour and mix on a slow speed until it forms a smooth paste. Do not overmix. Wrap in clingfilm and leave to rest in a cool place for at least an hour before use. Roll out to about 0.5cm (¼ inch) on a floured board. Cut with round pastry cutter into rounds which just overlap tartlet cases. Press pastry evenly into tins and trim edges. Prick bases. Cover and rest in the fridge for 30 minutes.

- BAKING: Bake for 10–15 minutes till the edges are beginning to colour a light golden brown. Remove from the oven. Put a tablespoonful of jam in each tart and return to the oven. Bake for another 5 minutes until the jam just begins to bubble – the pastry should now be cooked. Cool and serve with whipped cream.

Strawberry Tarts

Yield: 14–18

Pastry:

100g (3½ oz) unsalted butter

50g (2oz) icing sugar

1 egg yolk

175g (6oz) plain flour

Filling:

300ml (10fl oz) pastry cream (see p.122)

or

300ml (10fl oz) whipped cream

75g (3oz) melted best quality plain chocolate for brushing base (optional)

350g (12oz) strawberries

Strawberry glaze – see apricot glaze (p.126) and substitute strawberry jam

- Preheat the oven to 375°F/190°C/Gas 5. Grease 14-18 x 5cm (2 inch) tartlet cases.

- MAKING THE PASTRY: Beat butter and sugar in a mixer (or blend in a food processor) till light and fluffy. Add the egg and beat for a minute to mix in. Add the flour and mix on a slow speed until it forms a smooth paste. Do not overmix. Wrap in clingfilm and leave to rest in a cool place for at least an hour before use. Roll out to about 0.5cm (¼ inch) on a floured board. Cut with round pastry cutter into 14–18 rounds which just overlap tartlet cases. Press pastry evenly into tins and trim edges. Prick base to prevent bubbling. Cover and rest in the fridge for 30 minutes.

- BAKING: Bake for 15–20 minutes till a light golden brown. Remove from the oven. Leave to cool. Brush insides with melted chocolate (optional). Fill with whipped cream or pastry cream and cover with strawberries. Make a glaze with the jam and brush over strawberries. Serve.

Other Desserts

Burnt Cream

'This custard can be baked in the oven or cooked in a pan. I prefer to cook it in a pan. But whatever the method, the top must have a layer of sugar which has been burnt to a crunchy layer of burnished caramel.'

Yield: 4 x 150ml (5fl oz) bowls or pots

75ml (3fl oz) milk

50g (2oz) caster sugar

6 egg yolks

275ml (9fl oz) double cream

1 vanilla pod

2 tablespoons caster sugar for caramelising

- MAKING MIXTURE: Put milk, sugar and egg yolks into a bowl and beat well with a whisk. Put the cream into a pan. Split the vanilla pod in half and scrape the seeds into the cream in the pan. Add the pod and bring the cream gently to simmering point so the full flavour of the vanilla is infused into the cream. Remove from the heat and leave to infuse for another 10 minutes. Remove the vanilla pod. Pour half the cream over the egg and sugar mixture, beating well, then pour it back into the pan with the remaining cream. Cook gently, stirring all the time till the mixture thickens. Strain and pour into pots.

- FINISHING: Cover the surface with sugar and caramelise under a hot grill or use a pastry blowtorch. Serve immediately.

Eclairs, Choux buns and Profiteroles

'Never open the door on these, they're like a soufflé and will drop if you let in any cold air.'

Yield: eclairs and buns 10–12,
small buns (profiteroles) 18–20

100g (3½ oz) unsalted butter
Pinch of sea salt
Pinch of sugar
250ml (9fl oz) water
150g (5½ oz) plain flour
4 large eggs

Filling and Icing:
300ml (10fl oz) whipping cream
175g (6oz) best quality plain chocolate, melted
25g (1oz) butter
Icing sugar for dusting

Alternative filling:
half whipped cream, half lemon curd (see p.125), finish with dusting of icing sugar on top

- Preheat the oven to 400°F/200°C/Gas 6. Grease baking tray.

- MIXING AND COOKING: Cut the butter into cubes and put into a pan with the salt, sugar and water. Heat to melt the butter and remove from the heat just before boiling point. Add all the flour and beat vigorously until the mixture thickens. Return to the heat and cut and turn the mixture until it is thoroughly cooked – about 1 minute – when it should leave the sides and base of the pot without sticking. Do not overcook or the pastry will crack when baked.

- ADDING EGGS: Put the mixture into a bowl and continue to cut and turn it for a minute. Add the eggs, one at a time, beating between each addition (if using mixer, blend mixture on a medium speed). Use immediately or cover and keep in a cool place till ready for use.

- SHAPING AND BAKING: Put mixture into a piping bag with a 2cm (¾ inch) plain tube and pipe onto the baking tray in long fingers for eclairs or rounds for buns. Alternatively, use two dessert spoons to shape and place on baking tray. Bake for 10–20 minutes, depending on size of buns, until risen and browned. To see if they're ready, tap on the base – they should sound hollow. Cut slits while hot and allow to cool.

- FINISHING: Fill with whipped fresh cream or lemon curd. Coat with chocolate melted with butter in a pan over hot water. Alternatively, dust with icing sugar.

Pavlova

'This is usually made in one large round, but it can also be made in individual portions, although you will need lots of oven space.'

Yield: 8

225g (8oz) caster sugar
4 egg whites
Pinch of salt
2 teaspoons cider vinegar
2 teaspoons cornflour

Filling:
350g (12oz) soft fruits in season soaked in 2 tablespoons crème de cassis or other liqueur
300ml (10fl oz) whipping cream

- Preheat oven to 350°F/180°C/Gas 4 for the first five minutes then reduce to 275°F/140°C/Gas 1. Line baking sheet with parchment or silicone.

- MIXING: Divide the sugar roughly into four. Put egg whites into a bowl with the salt and beat until stiff. Begin to add the sugar in four lots, beating well between each addition. Add the vinegar and cornflour. Continue beating. The mixture should now stand up in stiff peaks. Pipe or spoon onto a baking tray in one large round. Or pile in individual mounds.

- BAKING: Bake in a hot oven for five minutes then turn down the heat and bake for about 1½ to 2 hours till pale golden. Leave to cool, remove from tin and cover top with whipped cream and berries soaked in liqueur.

Meringues

'To stop meringues "weeping" take one tablespoon of caster sugar out and replace it with an ounce of icing sugar.'

Yield:15 large, 30 small

4 egg whites
225g (8oz) caster sugar
Pinch of salt

Filling:
300ml (10fl oz) whipping cream

Serve with fresh fruits in season

- Preheat oven to 275°F/140°C/Gas 1. Line baking tin with parchment or silicone sheets.

- MIXING: Whisk egg whites and salt till they form peaks and then add about half the sugar gradually in tablespoons, beating between each addition. Add remaining sugar gradually by hand and when mixed in, pipe onto prepared baking trays. Dust with caster sugar which will make them crisp.

- BAKING: Bake for 2 – 2½ hours when they should be firm and dry. Cool and fill with cream. Serve with fresh fruits.

Little Pots of Chocolate

'This was a Triangle dessert.'

Yield: 4–6 pots

225g (8oz) best quality plain chocolate

250ml (9fl oz) double cream

1 tablespoons rum or brandy

1 tablespoon espresso coffee

200ml (7fl oz) whipping cream, whipped

Garnish: chopped pistachio nuts or ground cinnamon

• MAKING AND FINISHING: Melt the chocolate in a bowl over a pan of simmering water. Leave until cool but not set. Beat the cream till stiff. Add the espresso and rum. Add a little to the chocolate and blend through. Add the chocolate mixture to the remaining cream and mix lightly. Spoon into pots, leaving a space at the top for the whipped cream. Leave to set and finish with whipped cream. Decorate with chopped pistachio nuts, or a dusting of ground cinnamon.

Trifle

'While a Victoria or egg sponge is the traditional base for this sweet, an interesting alternative is a festive Italian yeast cake (panettone) which gives a lighter texture while also adding its aromatic flavours.'

Yield: 8–10. Glass bowl: 1.5L (3pt).

125g (4oz) ratafia biscuits or macaroons

250g (8oz) Victoria or egg-batter cream sponge (see p.78)

4–5 tablespoons brandy or Madeira

3–4 tablespoons high-fruit strawberry jam

Custard:
6 egg yolks

40g (1½ oz) caster sugar (1)

500ml (18fl oz) milk

75g (3oz) caster sugar (2)

Cream:
300ml (10fl oz) whipping cream, whipped

2 tablespoons toasted flaked almonds

• MAKING THE BASE: Crumble the biscuits into the base and cover with sponge. Sprinkle with brandy or Madeira and leave to soak for a few hours or overnight. Cover with jam and spread evenly.

• TO MAKE THE CUSTARD: Put the egg yolks into a bowl and beat with sugar (1) till the mixture forms a white ribbon. Put the milk and sugar (2) into a pan and bring to almost boiling point stirring all the time to dissolve the sugar. Pour onto the egg mixture, stirring well. Return to the pan and cook very gently over a low heat, stirring all the time, until the mixture thickens and coats the back of the spoon. Remove from the heat. When almost cool, pour over sponge base.

• FINISHING: When custard is set, pour over cream and decorate with toasted flaked almonds.

Caledonian Cream

'This is a flavoured cream which is best made the day before for the flavour to develop.'

Yield: 4

125g (4oz) cream cheese

125ml (4fl oz) double cream

1 tablespoon bitter chip marmalade

4 tablespoons brandy or rum

2 teaspoons lemon juice

sugar to taste

2 sweet Spanish naval oranges

4–6 slices petticoat tail shortbread (see p.70)

- MAKING: Blend the cream cheese, cream, marmalade, 2 tablespoons of the brandy, lemon juice and sugar together in a blender till smooth. Add sugar to taste (this will depend on the sweetness of the marmalade). Remove skin and pith from oranges and segment. Place in the base of large wine glasses, reserving some for the top. Sprinkle with remaining brandy or rum. Pipe or spoon the cream mixture on top and finish with a few segments of orange. Serve chilled with petticoat tails shortbread.

Bread and Butter Pudding

'This old fashioned British pudding has become a fashionable dessert, first updated by Anton Mosimann at the Dorchester in London in the 1980s when he made it with a rich French brioche (see p.56). Sultanas or raisins can be substituted for currants, the bread can be spread with marmalade – the variations are endless.'

Yield: 4–6

50g (2oz) currants, washed and dried

1/2 grated nutmeg

175g (6oz) thin slices of bread, buttered

3 large eggs

1 egg yolk

125g (4oz) caster sugar

600ml (1pt) milk (or milk and cream)

- Preheat the oven to 350°F/180°C/Gas 4. Grease a 1.25L (2pt) pie dish.

- MAKING AND BAKING: Mix the currants with the nutmeg. Sprinkle a few of the currants in the base of the pie dish. Then layer the buttered bread and remaining currants on top. Put the eggs and egg yolk into a bowl and beat well. Add the sugar and milk and mix in till sugar dissolves. Strain over the bread. Leave for 1 hour for bread to soak up custard. Bake for 40–50 mins till risen and set. Dust with icing sugar. Serve hot or cold.

Hot Orange Soufflé

'A pudding which requires some careful timing since it must go straight from the oven to table for maximum effect.'

Yield: 6

50g (2oz) unsalted butter

50g (2oz) plain flour

1 tablespoon orange and lemon zest

100ml (3fl oz) milk

75g (3oz) caster sugar

150ml (5fl oz) orange and lemon juice (2 oranges, 1 lemon)

4 large eggs separated

2 extra whites

50ml (2fl oz) orange flavoured liqueur, brandy or rum

Icing sugar for dusting

- Preheat the oven to 375°F/190°C/Gas 5. Brush a 1.4L (2½ pt) soufflé dish with melted butter and dust with caster sugar.

- MAKING THE SOUFFLE: Put the butter in a pan and melt. Add the flour and stir in. Cook for a few minutes without colouring. Add the orange and lemon zest. Gradually add the milk, stirring all the time. Beat with a whisk once all is incorporated. Cook, whisking, till thickened and smooth. Remove from the heat and add the sugar, lemon and orange juice, egg yolks and liqueur, whisking well. Finally beat the six egg whites till stiff and fold carefully into the mixture.

- BAKING AND SERVING: Pour mixture into soufflé dish and bake for 30–40 minutes till risen and lightly browned. Dust with icing sugar and serve immediately before it falls.

Cold Lemon Soufflé
(Soufflé milanaise)

'A classic which has stood the test of time.'

Yield: 6

15g (½ oz) leaf or powered gelatine

2 large lemons, juice

3 large eggs

150g (5oz) caster sugar

300ml (10fl oz) whipping cream

2 tablespoons pistachio nuts, finely chopped

- Surround an 850ml (1½ pt) soufflé dish with a collar of greaseproof paper which should come at least 5cm (2inch) above the rim. Tie in place with string.

- TO MAKE: Dissolve gelatine in the lemon juice. If using powdered gelatine dissolve in 2–3 tablespoons of boiling water and add to the lemon juice. Whisk egg yolks and sugar over hot water until thick and creamy. Whisk in dissolved gelatine and allow to cool. Whisk egg whites to soft peaks (stop before they become too stiff). When the lemon mixture is at room temperature, fold in cream and then whipped whites. Pour into the soufflé dish and leave to set. When ready to serve, remove paper, coat sides in chopped pistachio nuts.

Strawberry Cream *(Bavarois aux fraises)*

'A popular 80s dessert which we made in the Albany.'

Yield: 6

15g (½ oz) leaf or powdered gelatine
3–4 tablespoons cold water
225g (8oz) strawberries, hulled
50g (2oz) caster sugar
2 tablespoon lemon juice
300ml (10fl oz) double cream

Pepper Berry Sauce:
125ml (4fl oz) fruit coulis (p.126)
Milled black pepper to taste

- TO MAKE: To dissolve, soak the gelatine in cold water for half an hour. If using powdered gelatine, dissolve in boiling water. Put the berries in a blender and puree. Pass through a fine sieve. Add the sugar and lemon juice. Add the gelatine and mix in carefully. Whip the cream and blend into the strawberry mixture. Pour into ramekins, small pots or into a large mould.

- TO FINISH: Chill in fridge till set. Turn out large mould. Serve with sauce.

Snow Eggs *(Oeufs à la Neige)*

'A light pudding which makes a good ending to a rich meal.'
Yield: 6

600ml (20fl oz) milk
100g (4oz) caster sugar
1 vanilla pod
6 large eggs, separated
200g (7oz) icing sugar

Topping:
2 tablespoons toasted flaked almonds

- PREPARING THE MILK: Put the milk into a pan with 50g (2oz) caster sugar. Slit the vanilla pod and scrape the seeds into the milk. Add the pod. Bring to the boil and leave to infuse for about 10 minutes. Remove the vanilla pod.

- MAKING THE MERINGUE: Beat the egg whites until they stand stiffly in peaks. Gradually beat in the icing sugar. Return milk to the heat and bring to simmering point. Take spoonfuls of the meringue and shape with two spoons into egg shapes. Drop into the milk turning so that they cook for about 1 minute on each side. When cooked, drain and put into a deep dish.

- MAKING THE CUSTARD CREAM: Beat the egg yolks with the remaining caster sugar – 50g (2oz) – in a bowl. Pour half the milk over the eggs and sugar, whisking well. Return to the pan and heat, gently stirring all the time till it thickens and coats the back of a spoon.

- FINISHING: Pour the sauce into a decorative glass dish. Place poached meringues on top. Sprinkle over toasted almonds and serve.

Creams, Icings, Sauces and Glazes

From the simplest bun glaze to the most complicated
buttercream, these are essential tools of the trade. Some are
complicated procedures but most are simple and easy to
make. Many can be made up in advance and stored for
several weeks in the fridge while others, such as Lemon Curd
and Apricot Glaze, have an even longer shelf life.

Pastry Cream *(Crème patisserie)*

'A must if you want to enhance your buns, pastry, bread...'

300ml (10fl oz) milk

1 teaspoon vanilla extract or 1 vanilla pod

75g (3oz) caster sugar

6 egg yolks

25g (1oz) plain flour

25g (1oz) cornflour

100ml (3½ fl oz) whipping cream, whipped

- TO MAKE: Put the milk into a pan and bring to the boil. If using a vanilla pod scrape out seeds and add pod and seeds to milk. Leave to infuse for at least ten minutes. Strain. Beat the egg yolks and sugar together till thick and creamy. Whisk in the flour and cornflour. Pour the heated milk over gradually, beating all the time. Return to the pan and heat gently stirring all the time with a wooden spoon. Once it begins to thicken, beat vigorously till it comes to a smooth thickened paste. Cook for a few minutes. Put into a bowl and dust with a little icing sugar to prevent a skin forming. Cover and store in the fridge. Beat in whipped cream and vanilla extract (if not using a pod) when ready to use.

Classic Buttercream *(Crème au beurre)*

'Less sickly sweet than other buttercreams, this classic baker's buttercream is made with an Italian meringue giving it a light, very creamy texture.'

Sugar thermometer: optional, or use cold water test (see p.38)

Italian meringue:
80ml (3fl oz) water

350g (12oz) caster sugar

25g (1oz) glucose

4 egg whites

500g (1lb 2oz) unsalted butter, softened

- COOKING THE SUGAR (Italian meringue): Put the water in a pan and add the sugar and glucose. Place over a moderate heat and stir till it boils. Brush down sides with a brush dipped in cold water. Increase the heat and bring to the boil. Insert sugar thermometer and when temperature reaches 110°C (soft ball when tested in cup of cold water), take off the heat. Meanwhile put the egg whites into a bowl and beat in electric mixer until stiff. Return the sugar to the heat and bring up to 121°C (firm-hard ball when tested in cup of cold water see p.38) remove from the heat. Set the mixer to its slowest speed and gently pour the sugar in a thin stream into the meringue. It must not run onto the whisks. Continue to beat at a higher speed until the mixture is almost cold (about 10–15 minutes).

- ADDING THE BUTTER: Before the meringue is completely cold, cut the butter up into pieces and add while mixing on a slow speed. Beat for about 5 minutes until the mixture is smooth and creamy. Can be stored in the fridge for a week in an airtight container.

Flavoured Buttercream

'A simply made silky, smooth buttercream which can be used on any cake.'

175g (6oz) unsalted butter, softened

250g (9oz) icing sugar

Flavouring options:

1 teaspoon vanilla extract

4 tablespoons milk

or

4 tablespoons liqueur, rum or brandy

or

4 tablespoons orange or lemon juice

or

50g (2oz) cocoa powder

4 tablespoons boiling water

- TO MAKE: Put the butter in the mixing bowl and beat till soft and fluffy. Add the flavourings and beat till mixed in. Add the icing sugar gradually until light and smooth.

Chocolate Cream (*Ganache*)

For a 25cm (10inch) round cake, to coat sides and top:

25og (9oz) best quality plain chocolate

250ml (9fl oz) double cream

- HEATING THE CHOCOLATE: Break the chocolate into small pieces and put into a double saucepan or into a bowl over a pan of simmering water. Stir as it melts, remove immediately it is melted. Heat the cream to hand hot and stir into the chocolate.

- FINISHING: Leave to cool until it begins to thicken a little but not too much. Put the cake on a rack. Pour chocolate on top of the cake and spread evenly with a large spatula over the top and sides. Shake before it sets to make a smooth surface.

Robbie Coltrane's American Frosting
with coconut and pecan nuts

1 x 410g can of evaporated milk
(410ml or 14fl oz)

275g (10oz) caster sugar

125g (4½ oz) butter

4 egg yolks, beaten

1½ teaspoon vanilla extract

200g (7oz) fine coconut

125g (4½ oz) chopped pecan nuts

4 tablespoons apricot jam

• TO MAKE: Put the evaporated milk, sugar, butter and egg yolks into a pan and simmer gently, stirring continuously, for about 12 minutes till golden brown and reduced. Add the vanilla extract. Add coconut and pecan nuts. Mix through. Cover the top and sides of the cake with the frosting. Rough up with a fork. Leave to harden and serve.

Custard Cream *(Crème anglaise)*

'A tricky sauce to make since it can curdle easily if the temperature is too high. If it begins to curdle remove it from the heat and pour it through a sieve which will remove the scrambled egg.'

6 egg yolks

40g (1½ oz) caster sugar (1)

500ml (18fl oz) milk

75g (3oz) caster sugar (2)

• TO MAKE: Put the egg yolks into a bowl and beat with sugar (1) till the mixture holds a white ribbon shape when whisk is trailed over surface. Put the milk and sugar (2) into a pan and bring to almost boiling point stirring all the time to dissolve the sugar. Pour onto the egg mixture, stirring well. Return to the heat and cook very gently over a low heat, stirring all the time, until the mixture thickens and coats the back of the spoon. Remove from the heat. Strain and use hot or cold.

Butterscotch Sauce

'A rich, sweet sauce which works particularly well served slightly warm with ices.'

125g (4oz) golden syrup

250g (8oz) soft brown sugar

125g (4oz) unsalted butter

300ml (10fl oz) double cream

• TO MAKE: Put the syrup, sugar and butter into a pan. Melt the butter and dissolve the sugar. Add the cream. Bring to a boil and cook over a slow heat to reduce, stirring all the time, for about 10–15 minutes until it thickens slightly.

Chocolate Sauce

'Like butterscotch sauce, this is excellent warm with ices, especially plain vanilla.'

200g (7oz) best quality plain chocolate
150ml (5fl oz) milk
2 tablespoon double cream
1 tablespoon sugar
25g (1oz) butter, softened

- TO MAKE: Break up the chocolate into small pieces and put into a pan over another pan of boiling water or in a double boiler. Stir until chocolate is melted. Put the milk, cream and sugar into a pan and stir well while bringing to the boil. Remove and pour into the melted chocolate whisking all the time. Take the pan off the heat and beat in the butter.

Lemon Curd

'As well as being a piquant spread for scones, pancakes and crumpets, this is a useful filling for small and large tarts. Mixed with some double cream it is also a good filling for choux buns (see p.94) or for a vanilla butter sponge (see p.77).'

Yield: To fill a 25cm (9¾ inch) baked pastry flan ring or 2 x 500g (1lb) jam pots

6 lemons, zest and juice
225g (8oz) caster sugar
8 eggs, beaten
175g (6oz) unsalted butter

- TO MAKE IN A DOUBLE BOILER: Put the lemons, sugar and eggs into a double boiler or in a large heatproof bowl over a pan of simmering water. Whisk well to mix thoroughly and dissolve the sugar. Add the butter. Cook, stirring occasionally until it thickens and coats the back of the spoon. Remove from the heat.

- TO MAKE IN THE MICROWAVE: Put the butter and sugar in a bowl in the microwave and cook uncovered until the butter has melted. Add the lemon juice and zest and stir to dissolve the sugar. Add the eggs and whisk everything together. Return to the microwave and continue to cook, taking it out every 60 seconds to give it a whisk and check on its thickness. It should coat the back of a spoon when ready.

- Strain, pot and cover when cold. Store in a cool place. Use as required. Will keep for 2–3 weeks.

Apricot Glaze

'Buy the best apricot jam you can get. The higher the concentration of fruit, the better the flavour.'

125g (4oz) apricot jam
2 tablespoons water

* TO MAKE: Place the jam and water in a pan and bring to the boil, stirring occasionally. Simmer for about a minute. Remove from the heat. Strain, cover and store.

Bun Glaze

50g (2oz) granulated sugar
50ml (2fl oz) water
1 teaspoon glucose
Squeeze of lemon

* TO MAKE: Put into a pan and bring to the boil. Boil for 3 minutes. Cool and use as required.

Stock Syrup

600ml (1pt) water
375g (13oz) caster sugar
40g (1½ oz) glucose
1 tablespoon lemon juice
1 tablespoon rum

* TO MAKE: Put ingredients into a pan and bring to the boil. Simmer to reduce a little and form a smooth syrup. Strain. Cool and keep in a bottle or jar and use as required. Can be used to glaze tarts and fruit flans. Reboil to use. Will keep for several months.

Fruit Coulis

Soft Fruits:
Strawberries, Raspberries, Blackcurrants, Blueberries

Hard Fruits:
Peaches, Apricots, Plums

400g (14oz) fruit
2–3 tablespoons water
Stock syrup (see below)
1 lemon, juice

* FOR SOFT FRUITS: Wash, drain, hull as appropriate. Put into a blender and blend till smooth. Remove and sieve. Add lemon juice and stock syrup according to taste and according to the sweetness of the fruit. Cover and store in the fridge. Use as required hot or cold.

* FOR HARD FRUITS: Wash and de-stone or core the fruit. Put into a pan and add a little water. Stew gently till softened, stirring occasionally. Remove from the heat and leave to cool. Pass through a sieve or puree in a blender. Add stock syrup and lemon juice according to taste and sweetness of the fruit. Sieve. Cover and store in fridge. Use as required either hot or cold.

Festive Baking, Petits Fours and Confectionery

Time to get out the sugar and spice in earnest. And to indulge in some exquisite little mouthfuls which add style to the baker's art. At One Devonshire, we created some original versions which became signature items. In particular the mince pies that Lulu loved so much, not to mention the butter tablet which caught Delia Smith's attention.

Christmas Pudding

'In all my years as a baker and pastry chef I have never made a better pudding than this. Because it is steamed for such a long time, it stores well so the flavour develops. It's also good cold, cut in slices. This is a German recipe and has no flour so is very rich.'

Yield: 6–8

100g (3½ oz) breadcrumbs

100g (3½ oz) beef suet, finely chopped

or

Atora brand, beef or vegetarian

150g (5½ oz) currants

150g (5½ oz) raisins

100g (3½ oz) soft brown sugar

50g (2oz) ground almonds

50g (2oz) mixed peel

50g (2oz) crystallised ginger, chopped finely

1 lemon, zest

1 orange, zest

100g (3½ oz) glacé cherries, chopped finely

3 large eggs, beaten

2 tablespoons whisky

125ml (4fl oz) stout

Size of pudding bowl: 850ml (1½ pt) with lid, well greased

- MIXING AND STEAMING: Put all the dry ingredients into a large mixing bowl and mix well. Whisk the eggs, whisky and stout together and pour on top of dry ingredients. Mix well. The mixture should be a soft dropping consistency. Pour into pudding bowl and smooth on top. Clip on lid. Place in a pan of boiling water which should reach three-quarters of the way up the side of the bowl. Steam gently for 4–6 hours. The longer it is steamed, the better the flavour. Serve immediately or leave to cool and reheat as required. Will keep for at least a year, well wrapped in greaseproof paper and foil, in a cool place.

- Serve with Brandy Butter

Black Bun

'This is the traditional Scottish Hogmanay Bun, always accompanied by a "dram" of whisky. It is very rich and "black" and improves with keeping.'

1kg (2¼ lb) currants and raisins

1 tablespoon freshly ground cinnamon

1 tablespoon freshly ground ginger

2 grated nutmegs

½ teaspoon ground cloves

½ bottle brandy

125g (4oz) ground almonds

2 tablespoons black treacle

175g (6oz) blanched almonds

2 cooking apples, grated

150g (5½ oz) plain flour

Savoury shortcrust pastry:

200g (7oz) unsalted butter

400g (14oz) plain flour

150ml (5fl oz water)

Pinch of salt

- SOAKING THE FRUIT: Put the currants and raisins in a pan with the spices and pour over the brandy. Mix well and place over a low heat. Heat gently till the aromas are released. Remove from the heat, cover and keep in a cool place overnight, (or longer, up to a week) stirring occasionally.

- Preheat the oven to 325°F/170°C/Gas 3. Line 2 x 1.5L loaf tins or 1 x 23cm (9 inch) deep cake tin with baking parchment or silicone.

- TO MAKE THE PASTRY: Put the butter into the mixer bowl (or blend in food processor) and add half the flour. Beat on a slow speed until this has combined into a soft paste. Add remaining flour, salt and water and mix at a slow speed till a smooth paste. Do not overmix. The mixture should be firm but pliable. Wrap in clingfilm and leave to rest in a cool place for at least an hour before use.

- TO MAKE THE BUN: Add the ground almonds, treacle, blanched almonds, grated apple and flour to the steeped fruit and spices. Mix thoroughly. Divide pastry into a ⅔ and ⅓ piece. Using the ⅔ piece roll out to about 8mm (⅜ inch) thick and use to line the tin(s). Overlap the top edges a little. Leave to rest in a cool place till the pastry hardens, about 30 minutes. Fill tin(s) with bun mixture, smooth on top. Turn in top edges of pastry over the bun mixture. Brush with water. Roll out lid(s) to fit the tins exactly, trimming edges to fit. Place on top. Press down to seal edges. Brush lightly with beaten egg. Prick all over with a skewer, through to the base of the tin. Leave to rest for 30 minutes.

- BAKING: Bake for 2–3 hours depending on size (the larger size will take 3 hours). Remove bun (buns) from their tins after 2 hours and continue baking, upside down, to ensure base is completely cooked. Cool completely. Wrap in cling film and foil and store for at least a week (or up to a year) – the longer the better. Serve in thin slices with whisky at New Year.

Christmas Cake

'I got this brilliant recipe from an old pastry book,
"William Barkers' Pastry". I also used it, without the
spices and treacle, for a rich fruit wedding cake.'

800g (1lb 12oz) currants

375g (13oz) sultanas

375g (13oz) raisins

150ml (5fl oz) brandy or rum

8 large eggs

500g (1lb 2oz) unsalted butter, softened

500g (1lb 2oz) soft brown sugar

550g (1lb 4oz) plain flour

2 teaspoons cinnamon

2 teaspoons mixed spice

½ grated nutmeg

1 lemon, zest

1 orange, zest

2 tablespoons black treacle

2 tablespoons milk

50g (2oz) glacé cherries, washed and dried

150ml (4fl oz) rum or brandy for 'maturing'
the cake

- SOAKING FRUIT: Soak the currants and sultanas in the brandy or rum, cover and leave overnight or up to a week in a cool place, turning occasionally.

- Preheat the oven to 350°F/180°C/Gas 4. Line a 25cm (10 inch) round cake tin or 23cm (9 inch square) or for half quantity of mixture use 1 x 22cm (8½ inch) round cake tin. Tie a double band of brown paper round the outside of the tin to protect the cake during the lengthy baking.

- HEATING THE EGGS: Put the eggs, still in their shells, into a bowl of very hot, but not boiling water, leave for 2 minutes to heat the eggs without cooking.

- MIXING: Put the butter and sugar into a bowl and beat till white and fluffy. Add eggs gradually, beating between each addition. Sift the flour and spices together. Stir in the flour gently. Add the fruit, orange and lemon zest, treacle which has been, mixed through the milk, and cherries and mix in by hand. Pour into the tin. Level the surface and bake for about 3–4 hours (22cm or 8½ inch tin will take 2-2½ hours). Test with a skewer for readiness when it should come out clean. Leave in the tin to cool. Do not remove lining paper. When cool, make holes in the cake with a skewer and pour over rum or brandy. Wrap in clingfilm and foil and store till required.

Christmas Cake Marzipan and Icing

Marzipan for 1 large size cake:

500g (1lb 2oz) ground almonds

125g (4oz) caster sugar

125g (4oz) icing sugar

2 large eggs

2 teaspoons lemon juice

1 teaspoons dry sherry

Vanilla extract, few drops

Ready to roll fondant icing:
For large cake 1kg (2¼ lb)
For small cake 700g (1½ lb

- TO MAKE: Put the ground almonds, caster sugar and icing sugar into a mixing bowl and blend together. In a separate bowl, beat the eggs with the lemon juice, sherry and vanilla. Add to the almond mixture in three lots, beating on slow speed between additions. (Or mix by hand: make a well in the almond mixture and add the egg mixture. Knead in the liquid till the mixture comes together.) Dust a working surface with icing sugar and knead till smooth. Cover and leave to rest before use.

- For 1 small cake: use half quantity marzipan

- APRICOT GLAZE: 125g (4oz) apricot jam; 2 tablespoon water. Place the jam and water in a pan and bring to the boil, stirring occasionally. Simmer for about a minute. Remove from the heat. Strain, cover and store.

- TO FINISH CAKE: Brush apricot glaze liberally over top and sides of the cake. Roll out marzipan to fit and cover sides and top of cake. Roll out fondant icing to fit and cover sides and top of cake. Decorate as desired.

Clootie Dumpling

'Lighter and less rich than a Christmas pudding. It's made with "surprises" for children (and adults) for traditional festive occasions. It's made in a "cloot" (Scottish for cloth) which gives the dumpling its "skin": a vital part of the eating experience. Alternatively it can be made in a pudding bowl.'

125g (4oz) self raising flour

175g (6oz) fine white breadcrumbs

125g (4oz) beef suet

Atora brand, beef or vegetarian

1 teaspoon baking powder

2 teaspoons each of: Ground cinnamon, Ground ginger, Grated nutmeg

175g (6oz) sultanas

175g (6oz) California raisins

2 tablespoons golden syrup

2 tablespoons black treacle

2 eggs

1 large cooking apple, grated

1 large carrot, grated

1 orange, zest and juice

Dusting:
plain flour

- Prepare cloth (cloot) 55cm (22inch) square white cotton or linen. Fill a pan with boiling water and add the cloth. Boil cloth for a few minutes. Lift out with tongs, spread out on work surface. While still hot, sprinkle evenly with a thick dusting of flour. Shake to disperse evenly over all the cloth, then shake off excess.

- Prepare 'surprises' or 'charms'. The most commonly used are: the coin, foretelling wealth; the button, bachelordom; the thimble, spinsterhood; the horseshoe, good luck. It's also common to use just a few silver coins. They are all wrapped in greaseproof paper before adding.

- TO MAKE THE DUMPLING: Place a grid or upturned saucer in the base of a very large pot to prevent the dumpling sticking. Put all the ingredients into a bowl and mix to a soft dropping consistency using more orange juice to mix if necessary. The mixture should be neither too soft (when it will crack on turning out) or too stiff (when it will be too heavy a texture). Add the 'surprises' and mix through. Pour into the centre of the cloth. Bring up sides making sure all the edges of the cloth are caught up. Tie with a string leaving space for expansion. Hold up the tied ends and pat the dumpling into a good round shape. Lower into pot of boiling water. It should come about halfway up the dumpling. Tie ends of string to the pot handle which will prevent the dumpling rolling over and water getting in at the top. This also helps to keep it a good round shape. Cover tightly with a lid and simmer gently for 4 hours, checking the water level regularly.

- TO TURN OUT AND SERVE: Fill the sink, or a large basin, with cold water and lift out the dumpling, holding it by the string. Submerge in the water and leave for 60 seconds. This releases the cloth from the dumpling skin. Move to a bowl about the same size as the dumpling. Cut string, open out cloth, hanging edges over the bowl edge. Invert serving plate on to the dumpling and turn over. Remove cloth carefully. It should come away cleanly. Put into a warm oven to dry off when the skin will turn a dark, shiny brown. Dust with caster sugar on top and serve with whipped cream, custard cream (*see* p. 124) or a bowl of soft brown sugar.

Mincemeat

'This is easy to make – once you collect the ingredients. It also improves with age. So is worth waiting for a year-old vintage.'

175g (6oz) beef suet, finely chopped

750g (1lb 10oz) raisins, sultanas, currants

125g (4oz) mixed peel

125g (4oz) soft brown sugar

125g (4oz) strawberry jam

1 teaspoon salt

1 tablespoon ground cinnamon

1 tablespoon ground allspice

1 tablespoon ground mace

1 grated nutmeg

½ teaspoon ground cloves

2 lemons, zest and juice

½ bottle Amontillado sherry

¼ bottle brandy

• TO MAKE: Combine all the ingredients in a large container (pot, bowl, earthenware crock, plastic container) which has a lid, or cover, and mix well. Cover well and leave in the container to mature for at least 1 month, preferably longer. Turn occasionally, and add more sherry and brandy as required. Pot and store. Use as required.

Mince Pies

'Lulu said these were the best she'd every tasted. She took some home to London with her. The method uses a sweet shortcrust base and a puff pastry top, which was chef Andrew Fairlie's idea. It makes for a lighter after dinner pie. If you make them very small they can be used for petits fours.'

sweet shortcrust pastry (see p.93)
200g (7oz) puff pastry (see p.94)
mincemeat (see p.133)
2 tablespoons brandy
1 beaten egg
1 tablespoon apricot glaze (p.126)

- Preheat the oven to 450°F/230°C/Gas 8. Grease baking tray.

- TO MAKE: Roll out shortcrust to 5mm (¼ inch) thick and cut into rounds with a cutter (size according to preference). Place on the baking tray and put in the fridge to rest. Roll out puff pastry to the same thickness and cut into rounds with the same cutter. Cut two slits in the middle of each round to allow the steam to escape. Rest in fridge.

- FINISHING AND BAKING: Remove shortcrust rounds from the fridge. Brush off excess flour. Brush with beaten egg and place spoonful of mincemeat in the centre. Put puff pastry circle on top and press down round the edges to seal. Brush with beaten egg. Put to rest for half and hour. Brush with egg again and bake for 15–20 minutes till golden brown on top. Dust with sugar and serve hot or cold. They may also be glazed with apricot glaze. Bring glaze to the boil and coat pies while still warm.

Mincemeat Cake

'A lighter alternative to a rich fruit cake, a Victoria sponge mixture forms the base of the cake which has a layer of mincemeat on top covered with a crunchy topping.'

250g (9oz) self-raising cake flour

250g (9oz) caster sugar

250g (9oz) butter, softened

1 teaspoon vanilla extract

4 eggs, beaten with 3 tablespoons milk

500g (1lb) jar mincemeat (see p.133)

1 tablespoon brandy

Crunchy topping:

75g (3oz) soft brown sugar

50g (2oz) plain flour

50g (2oz) butter

3 teaspoons ground cinnamon

125g (4oz) crunchy oat cereal

- Preheat the oven to 350°F/180°C/Gas 4. Grease or line cake tin 23cm (9 inch) round cake tin with removable base.

- MIXING THE SPONGE CAKE: Sift flour into a bowl and add sugar. Beat with an electric beater for about 30 seconds. Add butter and about three-quarters of the egg and milk mixture. Beat for about a minute till the mixture becomes light and creamy. Add the remainder of the egg mixture and vanilla and beat for another 30 seconds. Pour into prepared tin.

- MINCEMEAT/CRUNCHY TOPPING: Remove mincemeat from the jar, add brandy, then spoon on top of cake mixture, spreading evenly. Put the ingredients for the crunchy topping in a blender and pulse for a few minutes till they form fine crumbs. Sprinkle evenly over the mincemeat.

- BAKING: Bake for 60 minutes or until a skewer inserted into the centre comes out clean. Cool in the tin for 10 minutes, then turn out onto a rack. Dust with icing sugar.

PETIT FOURS
Langue Du Chat *(Cat's tongue biscuits)*

'This is a super, crisp biscuit. It takes 10 minutes to mix, 10 minutes to pipe and 10 minutes to bake. Can also be used as a decoration for a gateaux round the edge, or with ice cream.'

Yield: 40–60

100g (3½ oz) unsalted butter
100g (3½ oz) icing sugar
Few drops vanilla extract
2 large egg whites
100g (3½ oz) plain flour, sifted

• Preheat the oven to 450°F/230°C/Gas 8

• MIXING AND BAKING: Put the butter, icing sugar and vanilla into the mixing bowl and beat to a smooth paste. Add the egg whites in 3–4 additions, beating well after each addition. Add the flour and mix to a soft paste. If it is too stiff add more egg white. Put into a piping bag with a 5mm (¼ inch) round hole. Pipe in 5cm (2 inch) lengths about 2.5cm (1 inch) apart. Bake for 10 minutes until the edges are lightly browned. Store in an airtight tin

Almond Tuiles

'Light as a feather, these curved, crisp little biscuits are not difficult to make.'

Yield: 20–24

50g (2oz) icing sugar
1 egg white
1 egg yolk, beaten
50g (2oz) flaked almonds
few drops vanilla extract
1 teaspoon flour, optional

- Preheat the oven to 400°F/200°C/Gas 6. Use greased baking parchment on double thickness baking trays or bake on a greased silicone sheet 'silpat'.

- TO MAKE: Mix the icing sugar with the egg white and egg yolk. Add vanilla. Gently fold in flaked almonds and leave to stand for 12 hours. Stir frequently to prevent mixture from separating and spoon out little heaps onto baking trays, leaving space between to spread. Flatten with a wet fork.

- BAKING: Bake until coloured, about 10 minutes. Remove from the oven and shape immediately by placing over a curved surface such as a rolling pin for a few seconds then sliding off. Keep remaining biscuits warm and work as quickly as possible. Store in a cool, dry airtight tin.

Palmiers
(Pastry leaves)

'A bit of a fiddle to make but they make wonderful crispy little mouthfuls.'

Yield: 30-40

125g (4oz) icing sugar
125g (4 oz) puff pastry, chilled

- Preheat the oven to 475°F/240°C/Gas 9. Use baking parchment on doubled baking trays or bake on greased silicone sheet, 'silpat'.

- TO MAKE: Dust the baking surface with icing sugar. Roll out the pastry to a long strip. Fold in three, turn and roll out again. Put in the fridge to rest for at least 20 minutes.

- TO SHAPE 'SWISS ROLL' STYLE: Roll out pastry to 25 x 31cm (10 x 12 inch) 3mm (⅛ inch) thick. Brush pastry with cold water and dust with icing sugar. Roll up tightly, as for a swiss roll. Cut in two with a sharp knife. Wrap in clingfilm and store in fridge overnight.

- TO SHAPE 'LEAF' STYLE: Dust the pastry with icing sugar and roll out to a square about 34cm (13 ½ inch) and 3mm (⅛ inch) thick. Trim the edges and cut the square into two to give two rectangular strips. Brush with water and dust with icing sugar. Bring the two short ends into the middle and then fold over the two folded ends to make a piece of pastry with four thicknesses. Repeat with the other strip. Place in the fridge for a few hours or overnight to harden.

- BAKING: Cut each piece of pastry along the cut edge into thin strips about 5mm (¼ inch) wide. Dust board and pastry with icing sugar to roll out. For 'swiss roll' style shapes roll out pastry so they are elongated to form a leaf shape. Place on baking tray cut side down, about 6cm (2½ inch) apart. Dust with icing sugar before baking. Lift onto baking tray with palette knife. Bake for 7–8 minutes till they are light amber coloured. Transfer to a wire rack and lay out to cool. Serve on the day they are made as they do not keep.

Madeleines

'You need the correct "Madeleine tin" to make these little mouthfuls immortalised by Proust .'

Yield: 120

125g (4½ oz) unsalted butter

125g (4½ oz) caster sugar

2 eggs, beaten

1 lemon, zest finely grated

125g (4½ oz) self-raising flour, sifted

- Preheat the oven to 425°F/220°C/Gas 7. Grease and flour a Madeleine tin (a baking tin with Madeleine-shaped moulds. Available from specialist cook/pastry shops).

- MIXING AND BAKING: Beat the sugar and butter till white and fluffy. Add the whisked eggs in three lots, beating well between each addition. Add the lemon zest and flour and fold in, mixing to a smooth batter. Using a teaspoon fill the individual moulds. Bake for 10 minutes till risen and golden brown.

CONFECTIONERY
Butter Tablet

'This unique tablet depends on a rich blend of butter and condensed milk for its special flavour. I raise my hat to Mrs Mathieson who won a WRI championship with it and kindly gave me her recipe. Delia Smith remarked on it when we served it with shortbread and coffee after lunch.'

Yield: 32 pieces

Sugar thermometer: optional, or use cold water test (see p.38)

150ml (5fl oz) milk
175g (6oz) unsalted butter
800g (1lb 12oz) caster sugar
225g (8oz) condensed milk

- Use a large 3L (5–6pt) thick-based aluminium pot to make tablet. Line tray 18 x 27cm (7 x 10½ inch) with layer of tinfoil covered with layer of cling film. Place prepared baking tray in the freezer overnight.

- TO MAKE: Put milk and butter cut into cubes into the pan and melt. Add the sugar and stir to dissolve. When dissolved and beginning to simmer, add the condensed milk. Stirring all the time to prevent burning, simmer for about 9–10 minutes or until the mixture turns light amber in colour. To test for readiness: put a little in a cup of cold water and it should form a softball (116°C on sugar thermo-meter). Take off the heat, place on a wet cloth and beat until the mixture lightens a little in colour and begins to thicken and 'grain'. Do not allow it to become too thick or it will not pour well.

- FINISHING Pour into the chilled tray. Leave for 30 minutes to set. Cover with clingfilm and put in the freezer for 1½ hours. Take out. Remove from the tin and turn onto a cutting board. Leave for 10 minutes. Score the tablet into four squares with the heel of sharp knife. Break into four. Then score each square into three lengths. Break off each length. Score into cubes. Finally break into small cubes.

Vanilla Fudge

'A softer texture than tablet which is achieved by beating for longer after it is cooked.'

Yield: 45–50 pieces

Sugar thermometer: optional, or use cold water test (see p.38)

300ml (10fl oz) double cream
250g (9oz) unsalted butter
250g (9oz) glucose
1kg (2lb 4oz) granulated sugar
1 teaspoon vanilla extract

• Use a large 3L (5–6pt) thick-based pot. Line two trays 18 x 27cm (7 x 10½ inch) with layer of tinfoil covered with layer of cling film. Place in the freezer overnight.

• TO MAKE: Put cream and butter into at thick-bottomed pan and bring to a simmer. Add the glucose. Continue simmering and add sugar. Stir well to dissolve sugar. Simmer for about 9–10 minutes, stirring frequently, when it should turn light amber in colour. Test for readiness: put a little in a cup of cold water and it should form a soft ball. (116°C on sugar thermometer). Take off the heat, place pan on a wet cloth and beat until it begins to turn creamy and 'grain'. This is beaten for longer than tablet.

• FINISHING: Pour into the chilled trays. Leave for 30minutes to set. Then put in the freezer for 1½ hours. Take out. Remove from the trays and turn onto a cutting board. Leave for 10–12 minutes. Score with the heel of a sharp knife into four squares. Then score each square into three lengths and then into cubes. Break into pieces.

Chocolate Truffles

'These get their name from their similarity to the earthy fungus: dark, intense and a rare treat.'

Yield: 20–28

200g (7oz) best quality plain chocolate
75ml (3 fl oz) double cream
25g (1oz) unsalted butter, softened

• TO MAKE: Put the cream into a pan and bring to the boil. Break the chocolate up finely (this can be done in the food processor). Remove cream from the heat and add chocolate, stir until the chocolate is melted. Add the butter and mix through. Pour onto a large flat plate and chill in the fridge until it is set and firm enough to shape.

TO SHAPE:
• Method 1: With a teaspoon, scrape across the chocolate to form a truffle 'curl' in the same style of a butter 'curl'. Roll in cocoa powder.

• Method 2: Immediately the mixture sets and before it hardens, put it into a piping bag with a 1cm (½ inch) nozzle. Line baking tin with clingfilm. Pipe into small rounds. Refrigerate for about an hour.

• Method 3: When the mixture is firm, use two teaspoons to shape into roughly oval bite-sized portions. Leave in rough shape or roll by hand into round balls, using cocoa powder to prevent sticking. Finish by rolling in cocoa powder.

Index